STUDIES IN MODERN EUROPEAN LITERATURE AND THOUGHT

General Editor:
ERICH HELLER
Profesor of German
in the University College of Swansea

HUGO VON HOFMANNSTHAL

Also published in this Series

Arturo Barea: UNAMUNO
E. K. Bennett: STEFAN GEORGE
W. H. Bruford: CHEKHOV
Roy Campbell: LORCA
J. M. Cocking: PROUST
Hugh Garten: GERHART HAUPTMANN
Rayner Heppenstall: LÉON BLOY
H. E. Holthusen: RILKE
P. Mansell Jones: BAUDELAIRE
P. Mansell Jones: VERHAEREN
M. Jarrett-Kerr, C.R.: FRANÇOIS MAURIAC
Janko Lavrin: GONCHAROV
Rob Lyle: MISTRAL
Richard March: KLEIST
José Ferrater Mora: ORTEGA Y GASSET
Iris Murdoch: SARTRE
L. S. Salzberger: HÖLDERLIN
Elizabeth Sewell: PAUL VALÉRY
Cecil Sprigge: BENEDETTO CROCE
Enid Starkie: ANDRÉ GIDE
J. P. Stern: ERNST JÜNGER
Anthony Thorlby: GUSTAVE FLAUBERT
E. W. F. Tomlin: SIMONE WEIL
Martin Turnell: JACQUES RIVIÈRE
Bernard Wall: MANZONI

Other titles are in preparation

HUGO VON
HOFMANNSTHAL

BY

H. A. HAMMELMANN

NEW HAVEN
YALE UNIVERSITY PRESS
1957

CONTENTS

'Poets in honour of the truth should write,
With the same spirit brave men for it fight.'

(Otway: *Venice Preserved*, Epilogue)

By one of those terrible over-simplifications and misreadings of history to which the recent past appears to be more liable than remoter periods, Imperial Vienna seems for ever cast in the musical comedy part of gaiety and romance, of dazzling uniforms and carefree music, of gentlemen and ladies of the old school in exquisite period clothes dancing, courting, flirting to the tune of Lanner's and Strauss's waltzes. Whether or not the Viennese themselves are responsible for this fable, or whether it was imposed upon Vienna from without by foreign visitors determined not to look behind the facade of never-never-land, to those who experienced the closing half century of the Austro-Hungarian Empire at first hand a much more ambiguous picture presented itself. The gaiety of course was there, and so was the easy splendour of the Imperial Court, the flow of high spirits and happy inconsequence of the *beau mondé* where it became essential to keep up appearances at any price, and pleasant ones at that.

For the easy-going Viennese society, escape from vexation into distractions had become habitual, all but a trait of character. True, the double eagle, if it no longer spread its wings over a realm where the sun never set, still ruled from the upper reaches of the Vistula down to the shores of the Adriatic, and from Lake Constance to the Wallachian plains, but the patriar-chal figure of Francis Joseph, whose shadow lay over all these domains, possessed none of the compelling power of Charles V, his sombre ancestor. Vienna, her greatness 'at the confines where the ancient and modern Europe meet', gained as an outpost of Christian civilisation against the infidel; her proud position reinforced during the centuries when she served as mediator between East and West, between North and South, as exchange mart between rival trading systems and heterogeneous cultures; her dignity and lustre exemplified and enhanced by such figures as Prince Eugene of Savoy and Mozart, 'Papa' Haydn and Schu-bert, Vienna—there was no denying it—had lost her dynamism, had become complacent, slack, barren. The policy of her cabinets, throughout the nineteenth century, was synonymous all over Europe with the maintenance of the status quo at all cost, and even to this shadowy purpose they laboured in vain. From 1859 onwards it was plain to all that Austrian diplomacy had lost its proverbial deftness for recouping military defeat. A sluggish administration still held together the vast remains of the old Hapsburg possessions, threatened as was the whole top-heavy structure by international socialism on the one hand and by the rising nationalism of its component parts on the other, but it did so by dint of the inherent inertia of heavy matter rather than through any new impulse or continuing vitality.

Those Austrians who looked with pride upon the glorious past of the Danubian double monarchy and with love upon the familiar landscape with its mingling of nationalities and tongues, and who searched for a task for their generation, could discover little to encourage them in their own society while it 'muddled along' uneasily pending the death of the old Emperor. It was not merely the general decline in initiative as a precursor of political disintegration, but something worse: a general apathy towards creative, original effort which drove the young Viennese intellectuals into a despondent isolation and brought about the peculiar atmosphere that *fin-de-siècle* took on in Vienna. Young artists and writers no longer felt themselves supported by the community to which they belonged; for their aspirations there appeared to be no room in this overstocked museum, and what they had to say seemed liable to be drowned in the pretentious and at the same time sentimental cult of 'old Vienna' affected by certain sections of a complacent bourgeoisie. The age of the Baroque, with its constant endeavour, so symbolic of Austria's mission and greatness, to achieve unity and synthesis out of a multitude of free forms, had long ago given way to the Biedermeier period, apotheosis of the stodgy Bürger in his night-cap.

What followed was largely, if eclectically, imported from abroad, from Munich, from Paris, even from Berlin. In this climate of easy-going material prosperity and shifting social foundations the men of the rising generation felt themselves in a vacuum. Their sense of non-attachment led them either to what wa scalled in Barrèsian French and excellent Viennese a '*culte du moi*', or to a perplexed and despondent crisis of self-confidence equally detrimental to their development.

It is against this dispiriting background that the appearance of the sixteen year old Hugo von Hofmannsthal must be seen if we are to understand the ascendancy which he immediately established among his contemporaries. We have the words of Arthur Schnitzler, then already a man of some literary reputation, for the impression made by the gawky, nervous schoolboy with his hair cut in fringes straight across the forehead, as he read with his almost falsetto voice one of his lyrical pieces to a small circle of friends. 'After a few minutes', Schnitzler told Stefan Zweig, 'we suddenly pricked our ears and began to exchange astonished, almost awe-struck glances. Verses of such perfection, of such faultless cast, suffused with so much musical glow we had never yet heard from a living poet, had hardly imagined possible after Goethe. Still more miraculous than this singular mastery of form', Schnitzler continued, 'unrivalled in the German language since that day, was the knowledge of the world which a boy not yet out of the classroom could have derived only from magical intuition. I felt that for the first time in my life I was in the presence of genius, and never again have I had this impression with such over-powering intensity.'

The little work which gave so overwhelming a proof of Hofmannsthal's prodigious early maturity, indeed completeness as a poet, and placed him, in the enthusiasm of his generation, at once almost with the immortals, with Keats and Rimbaud, with Novalis and Leopardi, was the 'lyrical drama' *Gestern*. *Gestern* is among the very earliest of Hofmannsthal's surviving poems and, I believe, the very first in point of time which he was willing to include in his own final collection of his poetry. The subject of this short verse play is the sad and tender bitterness of adolescence, its diffident shrinking from all ties and commitments. Only complete surrender to the mood of the moment, to the to-day, seems to promise enjoyment of all the beauty which life offers and of its pleasures, yet the young hero must learn, in disenchantment, that the yesterdays are ever with us, clogging the flight with *amères regrets:*

> Das Gestern ist so eins mit Deinem Sein,
> Du kannst es nicht verwischen, nicht vergessen:
> Es ist, solang wir wissen dass es war.
> . . . . . .
> Was einmal war, das lebt auch ewig fort.

> So much is yesterday part of your mind,
> You cannot wipe it out, cannot forget it:
> It is, while we have knowledge that it was.
> . . . . . .
> And all that once has been lives on forever.

If the story, Andrea's betrayal by his mistress, is commonplace and trivial, it is rendered poignant by the dignity with which the characters accept the inevitable dénouement. In any case, however, Hofmannsthal is not concerned with a sequence of

9

events, but with a mood out of which he weaves the pattern of his poem. It is the mood of his time. Here is the fastidious search for exquisite personal pleasures, but also, coupled with it, nameless misgivings, *Weltangst,* the fear that, in all this refinement of pleasure, the essence of life, so desirable and so elusive, may pass the poet and his generation by:

> Weil eine Angst nur ist in meiner Seele:
> Dass ich das Höchste, Tiefste doch verfehle.

> One fear there is that holds my soul in clasp:
> The utmost heights and depths elude my grasp.

It is fear—the young poet's insight is intuitive rather than experienced—which makes man a slave of time, as the materialism from which he seeks to escape would prove him a slave of his body.

Together with this high degree of consciousness we find in *Gestern* another of the young Hofmannsthal's outstanding characteristics, his faculty so to saturate his sensibility with other lives and forms of existence as to achieve a kind of self-identification. He feels with women in their inconstancy, reads in their eyes the desire to surrender and enjoy the never-tasted, the forbidden, the mysterious search, the restless yearning:

> Ich kann so gut verstehen die ungetreuen Frauen.
> So gut, mir ist, als könnt ich in ihre Seelen schauen,
> Ich seh in ihren Augen die Lust, sich aufzugeben,
> Im Niegenossenen, Verbotenen zu beben . . .
> . . . .
> Ich seh ihr Lächeln und die törichten, die Tränen,
> Das rätselhafte Suchen, das ruhelose Sehnen . . .

> I can so well understand these faithless women.
> So well indeed as if I peered into their souls,
> In their eyes I see the desire to surrender,
> To tremble in forbidden, never-tasted joys . . .
> . . . .
> I see their smiles and foolish tears,
> The mysterious quest, the restless yearning . . .

Hofmannsthal has the effortless capacity to step out of himself into other beings and speak with their voices. Here he is the Emperor of China:

10

In der Mitte aller Dinge
Wohne ich, der Sohn des Himmels.

In the centre of all things
I reside, the Son of Heaven.

Here the prisoner, the ship's cook:

Stille Tiere muss ich schlachten,
Schöne Früchte muss ich schälen
Und für sie, die mich verachten,
Feurige Gewürze wählen.

Quiet animals must I slaughter,
Perfect fruit cut into slices
And for those who have enslaved me,
Choose the fieriest of spices.

Now it is the cup of wine spilled by throbbing hands which
betrays the lovers' desire; now the old man, shivering in the
March storms, who feels the hand of death upon him and longs
for the summer, for the soothing night wind which brings him
no message of ill portent; here he is the madman among the
'happy few' of *Das Kleine Welttheater* who has unspeakable
knowledge of a higher order of things.

Hofmannsthal's vision is always directed towards the world
of the spirit, but the associations on which he relies and the
images which he uses to bring it close are never abstract or
remote. The splendour and wealth of his language, where he
chose to employ it to the full, as in a poem like 'Leben':

Mit schweren, reichen, purpurnen Gedanken

... with heavy, rich, and purple-coloured thoughts

or in *Der Tod des Tizian* consists rarely in an accumulation
of far-fetched words and complex metaphors; it is achieved,
on the contrary, through the sureness of touch with which, in
Hofmannsthal's own charming comparison, the poet does with
words what the gardener does with his shrubs and bushes:
'he places them, and combines them, in such a manner that
they appear at once new and strange, and yet for the first time
truly themselves, re-called to their true selves'. The poet's
incessant labour, he wrote, is 'the search for harmonies in
himself, a harmonising of the world which he carries within
him. In his supreme hours he need but find connections and
what he connects falls into harmony.'

11

'Zusammenschauen', as he called it, unity of vision both in space and time, was his true and, in the degree to which he possessed it, his exceptional gift, at first coming to him spontaneously, later as a result of a highly deliberate and responsible search for 'connections'. The transience of existence, the fleeting encounters and the loneliness of life, the growth of new generations into an inscrutable future, 'the land of the eternal seen in the unsteady light of the precarious hours between night and morning', these are the themes round which all his finest poetry is centered:

Dies ist ein Ding, das keiner voll aussinnt,
Und viel zu grauenvoll, als dass man klage:
Dass alles gleitet und vorüberrinnt.

This is a thing beyond all contemplation
And far too horrible for vain lament:
That all is gliding, all is in mutation.

Almost all the poems which Hofmannsthal himself cared to publish and to preserve were written between his seventeenth and his twenty-third year of age, a period which he himself described as the 'most lonely' of his life. During these years, in an adolescent stage to which he later gave the term 'pre-existence', he was able to see order and coherence where we commonly perceive only the individual concrete personal experience. An understanding with inanimate objects, which opened a vision transcending all experience of the senses, might be kindled suddenly by a breath of wind, by the sight of a tree or a Greek vase, even (as in the 'Chandos Letter') by a battered watering can. In this semi-mystical state the limitations of time, place and consciousness, the force of gravity to which man is subject, seemed to be overcome; the borderline between the finite and the infinite was temporarily suspended and he felt himself freed from the burden of the here and now. This momentary suspension appears in Hofmannsthal's poetry frequently as a dream. Thus, developing in the third 'Terzine' the lines: 'we are such stuff as dreams are made of', he sees dreams ever alive and present in our reality, revealing to us our true selves:

Wir sind aus solchem Zeug wie das zu Träumen,
Und Träume schlagen so die Augen auf
Wie kleine Kinder unter Kirschenbäumen
. . . . . .

12

Das Innerste ist offen ihrem Weben;
Wie Geisterhände in versperrtem Raum
Sind sie in uns und haben immer Leben.
Und drei sind Eins, ein Mensch, ein Ding, ein Traum.

Such stuff as dreams are made of, such are we,
And dreams open their eyes through the deep night
As children do beneath a cherry tree
. . . . . .
Like phantom fingers in a shuttered room
They are within us and are never done.
The inmost of our being is their loom;
A man, a thing, a dream, these three are one.

Out of such moments of elevation, the most important of
Hofmannsthal's lyrical poems seem to have sprung; they are
never a recollection of what actually was, but rather perhaps a
foreshadowing of what will be, a visionary anticipation of life
and death as in 'Ballade des äusseren Lebens', where the theme
of isolation, the vanity and evanescence of life is still further
developed:

Und Kinder wachsen auf mit tiefen Augen,
Die von nichts wissen, wachsen auf und sterben,
Und alle Menschen gehen ihre Wege.

Und süsse Früchte werden aus den herben
Und fallen nachts wie tote Vögel nieder
Und liegen wenig Tage und verderben

with its elegiac solace

Und dennoch sagt der viel der 'Abend' sagt,
Ein Wort, daraus Tiefsinn und Trauer rinnt
Wie schwerer Honig aus den hohlen Waben.

And children grow with wide and wondering eyes
That know of nothing, they grow up and die,
And every man pursues his lonely path.

And bitter fruit turn ripe and sweet, and lie
Like dead birds in the grass when they are shed
during the night, and soon they rot and dry.
. . . . . .

13

And yet he does say much who 'evening' says,
A word from which sadness and meaning flow
As honey trickles from the hollow comb.

Nowhere did Hofmannsthal realise and express this immanent awareness of the essence of existence more perfectly than in his famous poem, 'Ein Traum von grosser Magie', where rhythm and diction move with an airy, gliding, evanescent lightness which leads almost imperceptibly to a splendid, magic vision of a higher, timeless reality:

Viel königlicher als ein Perlenband
Und kühn wie junges Meer im Morgenduft
So war ein grosser Traum — wie ich ihn fand
. . . . . .
Cherub und hoher Herr ist unser Geist —
Wohnt nicht in uns, und in die obern Sterne
Setzt er den Stuhl und lässt uns viel verwaist:

Doch Er ist Feuer uns im tiefsten Kerne
— So ahnte mir, da ich den Traum da fand —
Und redet mir den Feuern jener Ferne
Und lebt in mir wie ich in meiner Hand.

More regal still than pearl and diamond
And bold as youthful sea in morning air,
Such was a great dream that one night I found.
. . . . . .
Seraph our spirit is, and lord anointed,
Stays not in us, but sets his chair before
The topmost stars and leaves us disappointed:

Yet he is fire within our inmost core
—Dimly my dream helped me to understand—
Conversing with the fires on yonder shore
And lives in me as I live in my hand.

Poems such as this cannot be interpreted by setting one symbol for another. They must be experienced; but if they meet the reader at a receptive moment, they achieve what Hofmannsthal believed to be the function of true poetry: 'to touch strings and strike harmonies which have been asleep in us without our knowledge, so that we look into the depths of wondrous mysteries as if a new meaning of life were opened to us'.

Inevitably perhaps, the early super-sensitivity which enabled, indeed impelled the young Hofmannsthal at times to immerse himself so completely in a world outside his own existence appears to be accompanied by a sense of aloofness and detachment, amounting almost to passivity. The gift, as he himself recognised when he spoke at one stage deprecatingly of his 'chameleon-like attitude', of his 'lack of character' even, is a great, but dangerous one; it is the one which, above all others, has caused him to be dubbed an aesthete, a 'pure' poet concerned only with aesthetic effects. Only later did Hofmannsthal himself fully understand his position when, in his essay 'Der Dichter und diese Zeit', he called the poet, by one of his happiest images, 'the silent brother of all things'. For, from the very outset, the detachment was not by any means the detachment of unconcern, but evidence, on the contrary, of a desire, and the ability, to step back at times, or upwards out of a bewildering world to a point of vantage from where the eye, surveying the human scene, commands a comprehensive view. There the wider implications reveal themselves and the universal becomes apparent beyond the particular, the particular takes its place in a larger framework:

> Manche freilich müssen drunten sterben,
> Wo die schweren Ruder der Schiffe streifen,
> Andre wohnen bei dem Steuer droben,
> Kennen Vogelflug und die Länder der Sterne.
>
> Manche liegen immer mit schweren Gliedern
> Bei den Wurzeln des verworrenen Lebens
> . . . . . .
> Ganz vergessener Völker Müdigkeiten
> Kann ich nicht abtun von meinen Lidern,
> Noch weghalten von der erschrockenen Seele
> Stummes Niederfallen ferner Sterne.
>
> Viele Geschicke weben neben dem meinen,
> Durcheinander spielt sie alle das Dasein,
> Und mein Teil ist mehr als dieses Lebens
> Schlanke Flamme oder schmale Leier.

> Some it is true must perish down below
> Where the heavy oars of the ships brush by,
> Others have their place up by the helm,
> Knowing flight of birds and lands of stars.
>
> Some lie permanently heavy-limbed
> At the roots of darkly tangled life
> . . . . . .

Weariness of quite forgotten races
I cannot brush off my eyelids,
Nor hold away from the startled soul
Silent falling of distant stars.

Many fates are spun along with mine
Inter-mixed and shuffled all by Destiny
And my share is something more than this life's
Tenuous flame or slender lyre.

In his poetry Hofmannsthal probably never came closer to an
elucidation of the constant interplay of time, and of the infinitude
of identity of which he was aware, than in these two closing lines:

Und mein Teil ist mehr als dieses Lebens
Schlanke Flamme oder schmale Leier.

Twenty-six poems out of a production of little more than five
years were all that Hofmannsthal selected and retained when
he prepared the last edition of his works published in his
lifetime: a minute fraction of his life's literary output. With
scarcely half this number of poems he had made his sensational
rise to fame in the eighteen-nineties. Today the precocity no
longer concerns us, nor the awe-struck astonishment which it
produced among his contemporaries; the sensational element
of the young Hofmannsthal's sudden rise is little to posterity,
but the assurance of his mastery remains, and with it his place
among the great lyric poets of the German language. Yet
perhaps the most weighty part of his work and of his legacy to
later generations was still to come.

II

Hofmannsthal was barely in his middle twenties when he became
aware of a drying up, perhaps an exhaustion of that abundant
lyric gift which during his adolescent years had poured itself
into the world 'like a gushing mountain stream'. It was a
cessation no less over-powering than the splendid, precipitate
effusion of his early genius. The intuitive certainty of the harmony
of the universe seemed lost and with it that state in which it was
manifest to him that human beings, 'animals, trees, clouds,
stones, all are the living mysterious hieroglyphics, the characters
with which God has written unspeakable things into the

world . . ., characters which language cannot interpret', but whose mystery the poet can feel and convey. We know from Hofmannsthal's letters how gravely bewildered and threatened he felt by this stagnation of his creative powers, aggravated as it was by corroding doubt about the efficacy of language itself. The crisis—which has been called the crisis of modern consciousness, for other poets, too, were to experience this loss of all true reality and mistrust of the adequacy of words where every generalisation appears undemonstrable, mendacious and hollow as soon as it is uttered or written,—was not a sudden onslaught. As early as 1896 the poet wrote to Stefan George of his doubts 'whether I have any right whatever to allow words with which we denote values and judgments to pass my lips', and more than five years later he told his friend Rudolf Alexander Schroeder of his efforts to regard this continuing paralysis in the light of an 'uneasy, laborious transition from the fertility of adolescence to that of manhood, a process of profound transformation of mind and spirit outwardly characterised merely by pain and torpor'.

It was when he had reached this point that Hofmannsthal was able, in writing his famous imaginary 'Chandos Letter' (August 1902), to face and state, and in this way to overcome, his experience. Lord Chandos, a young Elizabethan nobleman of great intellectual attainments and exactly the author's own age, in an imaginary letter to Lord Chancellor Bacon, explains to his paternal friend the reasons for his complete abandonment of all literary pursuits. He describes a most terrifying crisis, one taken from Hofmannsthal's own inner life, a vital experience: the complete loss of the ability to think or speak coherently on any general subject and to utter even casual opinions and judgments because he has been seized by a paralysing doubt about the adequacy of the language he must use: how, at first, he began to feel an inexplicable distaste for abstract terms and generalizations until he found himself unable any longer to comprehend human beings and their actions with the simplifying eye of habit; everything disintegrated into parts and words 'congealed into eyes staring at me and forcing me to stare back, whirlpools leading into the void which made me reel'.

The predicament of Lord Chandos is told by Hofmannsthal with great force in a succession of immediate and startling pictures and with unrelenting sharpness of focus; the haunting conviction carried by this important smal prose piece brings out in strong relief the closeness of the experience to the poet

17

himself, which had been, and obviously still was, almost an obsession. For all that, the situation of Chandos is not wholly his own: the very writing of this imaginary letter shows that it was rather an imagined extreme possibility of a state of mind recognised as temporary. Here the problem of communication crystallises itself. The inexplicable distaste, even 'hatred', is the product of a double scruple, a two-fold pressure unrelieved: on the one hand moral disgust, a strong sense of intellectual honesty outraged by the misuse of words and unconsidered judgments on the part of others; but also, no less grave, mistrust, nagging, crippling mistrust in the adequacy of words, his own words even, to convey to others the meaning they are intended to communicate. It is a problem which was to recur again and again in Hofmannsthal's later work, not least in his comedy *Der Schwierige*. Kafka has a parable of royal messengers rushing ceaselessly through the world and shouting to each other messages which have no meaning because the monarchy has long been abolished; where common premises have gone by the board, communication becomes purely fortuitous.

The exhaustion of his own productivity as a poet thus appears to have struck Hofmannsthal as a sign, a symbol of the extinction of our civilisation, of the climate in which the poet can still create and communicate. Although profoundly disturbed and alarmed by the phenomenon, he was able to rise superior to this most terrible experience of stagnation and to explain, in the 'Chandos Letter', the reasons why his voice as a lyrical poet might not be heard again. But while Lord Chandos confesses himself condemned to complete silence, Hofmannsthal was too deeply aware of his duty as a man and artist to allow himself resignation. For many years he continued to hope (in vain as it turned out) that 'out of this new state of mind new poems might emerge, equally pure and strong but quite different from the early ones, and they will perhaps still emerge, but for these I am probably not yet ripe'. But even though this one way of expression was sealed to him, he sought and found another.

If the exhaustion of our civilisation as a living, universal binding force was a cause, perhaps a predominant cause of the cessation of his own creative capacity as a poet, it was so because Hofmannsthal's sensitiveness was so extreme, so 'seismographic', his precarious adjustment to the world in which he lived and worked so nicely balanced that, even a decade and more before the collapse of the old Europe, the signs he saw, mere warnings of the storm to others, oppressed him as presages of the near-

18

inevitable. In the years which followed the 'Chandos Letter', years in which he gradually overcame his deep discouragement and nervous crisis, he not merely took stock of individual symptoms of the decay of European tradition—fragmentation, the relativity and subjectivity of the word as a means of communication, the lack of coherence—but became increasingly conscious of its causes. In the Austro-Hungarian Empire, close at home, behind the capital with its facade of brilliance and *joie de vivre*, there lay a hinterland whose political and cultural illiteracy told its own tale. Culture means living tradition, where art finds its natural place in the life of the community, a community conscious of and alive to its past as an obligation for the future, not dully worshiping that which it has allowed to die. It was the realisation that art separated from life is the very symptom of the end of a civilisation, and his recognition of his own duty as an artist to keep it alive, which removed Hofmannsthal from the very outset from all literary cliques, made him more and more unwilling to be drawn into the circle around Stefan George and determined to seek his own way in a diametrically opposite direction.

It is the real significance, from the point of view of Hofmannsthal's development, of his meeting and prolonged if somewhat uneasy correspondence with Stefan George that, in the face of the constant pressure which George exercised on him to draw him over to his own unbending views on art and life, the younger man was forced to clarify his own position. George, intent, single-minded and taut as he was, appears to have cut a somewhat incongruous figure in the relaxed atmosphere of Vienna. For all that, the singular attentions of one of the few living poets whom he regarded as his equal, and whose striving for integrity and perfection was no less uncompromising and severe than his own, must have presented a real temptation to the young Hofmannsthal. In an essay on George written in 1896 Hofmannsthal speaks of George's 'wonderful way, the only possible way, to hold the powers of life for nothing in the portentous knowledge of the singleness of destiny', and again: 'So completely mastered is life in these poems, so conquered, that incredible peace and the cool stillness of a dark temple soothes our noise-racked senses. We are in a grove, an island sundered from the ways of men by the cool defiles of immense silence'. Something not so very different seems to be aimed at in Hofmannsthal's own *Der Tod des Tizian*.

The temptation to make of one's limitations a manner, and

19

of that manner a law, is a grave one; that Hofmannsthal was able to overcome it, with such firmness, shows how early he saw the true road of his necessary development taking him in a very different direction. At one stage in the correspondence between the two poets, George speaks of his endeavour 'to establish a salutory dictatorship in our literature'; 'that this did not come to pass', he complains with bitterness, 'is your responsibility'. It was a charge which could hold no sting for the Austrian who sought not exclusiveness and domination, but on the contrary assimilation and integration. While George fenced off his work and that of his disciples to protect their impeccability and to keep out all others, the 'non-artists', Hofmannsthal became increasingly aware that poetry must be an essential, integral part of life within the community until, with that 'social willingness' of which Jacob Wassermann has spoken, he wrote to George outright that he saw the vocation of the poet in a 'mingling with the throng', in 'that speaking to the crowd, into the crowd, which is the duty of each artist in his own sphere'.

The exhaustion of Hofmannsthal's early lyrical gift thus coincided with a growing recognition that for an artist isolation, however splendid, must inevitably lead to sterility. He began to realise that the loneliness and the pessimism, no less than the *Weltangst* of his adolescence were all one, and had their roots in tragic non-attachment to that which was close at hand. In his *Buch der Freunde,* a collection of aphorisms and short, carefully formulated observations rather similar to Novalis, we find this sentence: 'German intellectuals are born to real life late and with heavy labour; that is when they undergo a second birth during which many die'; a remark whose autobiographical nature is made fully explicit in the private meditation on his own development as an artist which he jotted down under the title *Ad Me Ipsum.* Hofmannsthal knew that man can find himself only in seeking others.

In a twofold sense, this knowledge is already inherent in Hofmannsthal's early lyrical dramas, especially in *Der Tor und der Tod* (1893). This is the tale of the fool who only learns that he has wasted his life in eternal toying and trifling when death comes to fetch him—the first reality he has encountered. Claudio, the aesthete who surrounds himself with beauty, but cannot truly enjoy it, is detached from life, closed—as his name would seem to emphasise—to all true experience, for fear of the pain it may bring to him and of the pain he might inflict on

20

others by action; he becomes aware too late that he cannot enjoy the world without suffering and that the most cruel pain is that inflicted by indifference, by coldness of the heart.

The closing lines of *Der Tor und der Tod*, which celebrate death as a mystical experience, are taken up again in the last of Hofmannsthal's lyrical dramas, *Das Bergwerk zu Falun*, which he never published as a whole and probably never considered finished. The theme is the search for greater awareness, symbolised in a miner who abandons action, power and human love, and chooses the uncertain way into the dark shaft whose end is unknown: death and what may be beyond. In contrast to Novalis, from whom the picture of mining as the school of inner freedom is obviously taken, Hofmannsthal's hero, Elis Froebom, does not yet know what he seeks; he is merely aware that he seeks. He realises that he can reach the Mountain Queen only by complete self-surrender and liberation from all desire; yet, when the full vision is granted to him and the Queen lifts her veil, all we learn is that Elis stands blinded by her beauty and sinks to his knees. Nothing is vouchsafed us of what he has seen and it is at least open to question whether Hofmannsthal's inability to say anything significant does not reveal the blank by which he himself was faced.

Das Bergwerk zu Falun is interesting chiefly as marking the furthest point to which the poet went in the attempt to find an answer in direct mysticism. The shaft into which he descended proved a *cul-de-sac* not so much perhaps because he was incapable of the self-abandonment, the self-immolation which is required, but because he was too honest to pretend, even to himself, that he had found at the bottom of the pit anything but the silence of withdrawal. This is the turning point at which Hofmannsthal appears to have finally abandoned the isolation of mysticism and to have recognised that man needs the world in order to understand what he is, to realise himself in action and suffering. With the knowledge that action within the social context is for the non-mystic the most immediate way to the 'higher self' which he sought, he stepped out of the aloofness and seclusion of his adolescence and found his true road in acceptance of his commitment to the community and to tradition.

This endeavour to create for himself a larger audience is the motive force of Hofmannsthal's transition from the lyric poet to the writer for the stage, for the theatre, in the opening years of the present century. He himself described as 'the conquest of reality' the long period of search and experiment which proved to him, solitary and exclusive as he was by reason of his extreme sensitivity, in many ways a difficult and anxious one. Yet it was plain that, whether or not art was losing its basis and essential place in modern life, he himself had placed his own on too narrow a basis. His poems, as he knew, could count on no more than a few hundred readers; his lyrical dramas, though performed once or twice, were utterly unsuited for the stage, cast as they were essentially in monologue form, as if to emphasise the isolation in which the characters, and even their creator, moved.

The turn to sociability may lie in the smallest gesture. Significantly enough, it was in the 'Chandos Letter', document of utter dissociation, that Hofmannsthal adopted for the first time the method of using imaginary letters and imaginary conversations as an escape from the loneliness and isolation of self. More and more, as if to reassure himself that he is being understood, he seeks contact with an ideal recipient, an ideal listener; more and more he seeks the participation of others.

III

It has sometimes been suggested that it was the urge to create the *Gesamtkunstwerk* which led Hugo von Hofmannsthal to the theatre and consequently to opera. In fact the deliberate decision to devote himself to what he called 'this strange impure art form of the theatre', which brought him so much reproof and expostulation, was taken on grounds far more personal: here converge the fundamental problems of his own existence as an artist with his considered convictions about the place of the man of letters in the modern world. The premature period of his early poetic fecundity, in which it was given him to disappear in all manner of animate and inanimate objects and 'to speak out of them with their tongues'; when, in his mind's eye, what he saw was but a parable of something greater, and 'each creature but a key to all others'—this period, which he himself called 'pre-existential', ended before he had reached his twenty-fifth year. From then onwards, a point which he has marked in the 'Chandos Letter', Hofmannsthal's life and work was directed towards regaining, and restoring, by a conscious effort, that which, in his adolescence, had been his without asking: the vision of all existence as one great unity. His calling as a poet, his mastery over words for which one of his friends

22

found the telling phrase 'words obeyed him', always was to him a gift of responsibility; a calling not merely, but a command, a charge. For this charge he lived; unaffected by success, undeterred by failure, he carried it, carried it on, carried it out. With that 'social willingness' which had become manifest in his relations with Stefan George, he strove for the rest of his life to fulfil what he saw as his duty as an artist: to restore this harmony of life and imagination in himself and to communicate this healing knowledge of the essential wholeness of existence to those among whom he lived.

With a sensitivity which reacted to subtle currents and cross-currents of the social atmosphere, Hofmannsthal discerned clearly the ominous portents of disintegration in western civilisation, the threat of spiritual anarchy. To prevent the loss of the great European inheritance as a living, vital force and to preserve its values was his constant preoccupation. Hofmannsthal saw the solution of his own problem, and of the world around him, not in simplification, an ironing out of the concrete, ever-renewed conflicts, not in compromise, but in a living with and through these creative tensions, in the conquest, through action and suffering, of 'the higher', that point of vantage from which conflicts and discords fall into harmony again within a larger vision of the human condition.

'Two antonyms', he wrote in *Ad Me Ipsum*, 'were to be solved; that between individual loneliness and the community, and that between passing time and permanence'. To present the life of the individual in its commitment to the community and as part of the common human destiny; to show the passing moment as the very stuff, a minuscule yet pregnant part of eternity: this appeared to him as the true task of the poet, personal, pressing, urgent.

'The works and values of art', says the proclamation of the Salzburg Festival which Hofmannsthal composed at the end of the first world war, 'are the only lasting forces in the constant changes of time'. To preserve them and to fill them again with new life was to him the ever-renewed obligation of the artist. Convinced that the individual cannot produce anything of lasting and permanent value unless he bases himself, and builds on the tradition within which he lives, he refused to listen to that which obtruded itself upon him as the apparent 'demand of the day' and drew instead on the great treasures of our common European inheritance in his attempt to speak to modern audiences.

To say of one of the great masters of the German language, and one as familiar as Hofmannsthal with the best of the German literary tradition, that in this endeavour to recall his fellow men to their heritage the very words and conceptions began to appear inadequate and even refused to serve him, is almost a paradox. The inefficacy of language as a means of communication may be an old complaint; here, in the description of the young Lord Chandos, that the words he wished to use 'congealed' or 'crumbled in his mouth like mouldy mushrooms' is something more, something far more terrible: the suspicion that the very materials which the artist must handle to create an imaginative experience for others may have become too brittle, rotten, cankered in the general disintegration to serve his purpose. It is this suspicion which, at times, has led certain artists, and among them some of the greatest, to strike out on an entirely fresh road, seeking new possibilities, new materials, new forms.

Must the old be abandoned so that the new can take its place? Hofmannsthal was not an innovator in this sense: he saw his task in conservation, in keeping alive the legacy of earlier generations, and in filling with new spirit; he believed that each step forward, each new work of art, must be based on the foundations laid by the past. The debasing of language and of its values he countered by still greater care in its use, by avoidance of over-statement and glib generalisations; and so, in his later work, he found a prose style both simple and pregnant which is at the same time individual and yet formed on the great classic models. And equally, in his attempt to communicate that which he had to say, he did not search for new literary forms (though he did not disdain even to write scenarios for films in the early days of the cinema), but sought to employ those which had in the past proved the most universal media of expression and communication.

There is a suggestive sentence in the 'Chandos Letter' in which the writer says: 'I feel we might be able to enter into a new, clear-sighted relation to existence if we were willing to think with our hearts'. It was the attempt to express himself in a medium more direct, more fluent and more telling than words which led Hofmannsthal to pantomine and ballet, to drama and to the opera. The stage, which in mime and gesture reveals the unspoken and deeply hidden, and music, which makes directly felt that which is 'too vast, too true to be encompassed in words'—these were the means he wished to invoke to touch the imagination, the receptive and creative instincts of his fellow men.

It was almost inevitable in Vienna that the theatre should have moved Hofmannsthal from his youth. As early as 1892, the year in which he left school, he wrote for a periodical an account of the first visit of Eleonora Duse to the Austrian capital which draws a parallel between the week of her debut and the Great Dionysia in ancient Athens. The effect of the great actress on the public is described in terms such as these: 'Moods of different colour chased each other, and so long as we heard her, Duse struck chords in us only rarely touched by an artist, and then only by one who tears himself wide open . . . '. Hofmannsthal could hardly deceive himself that his own lyrical dramas, *Gestern, Der Tor und der Tod, Der Tod des Tizian,* though ostensibly written for the stage and occasionally performed, were of an order to arouse that kind of emotional experience. Indeed he had to become aware that they formed part of his lyrical output and could no more have a real place in the theatre than the essentially non-dramatic verse-plays which succeeded them, the oriental *Hochzeit der Sobeide* (1899) and *Der Abenteurer und die Sängerin* (1899).

So far from reviling the commercial theatre, or from blaming the stage and the public for the failure, he set himself the task of conquering theatre audiences with that to which they could and would respond. 'It is absurd to use the dramatic form and yet to be unwilling to have anything to do with the theatre', he wrote later, and it was a remarkable recognition for one who had for so long taken his cue from Browning's dramatic idylls and from Swinburne. 'If one concerns oneself with the theatre and steps before the public, one has made a decision; one acts because one intends to make an impression on the public.'

For the lyrical poet to win the living theatre is no easy matter, and Hofmannsthal's case was no exception. To know that the stage demands, as his friend Rudolf Borchardt put it, 'something less than poetry and something more than poetry' was not enough. For a long time the right key which would open the play-house and give him that access to the public for which he longed proved elusive. Only through constant application and perseverance over many years was Hofmannsthal able to make good the handicap of a more than devious approach. Before he could achieve this success, he had to learn a great deal, and he learnt it largely through the experience of failure. That the young essayist, who had seen behind the acting of Duse the

25

Dionysian festivals at Athens, should have hoped to gain the contemporary stage by reviving Greek tragedy, the tragedies of Sophocles, may seem understandable; the connection, however, was hardly close enough to save from failure his attempt to make *Electra* and *Oedipus* 'psychologically more convincing' to modern eyes. For all Hofmannsthal's ability to assimilate the spirit and the formal language of other ages, of Molière and Calderon, of the 'Arabian Nights' and even of medieval allegory, his conception of Greece—seen, one feels, through the eyes of the baroque—was altogether incommensurate to his task. As it happened, *Elektra* was turned by Richard Strauss into a masterpiece of music and even *Oedipus Rex* came in for a passing share of glory when Max Reinhardt, some years later, scored one of his more ambiguous triumphs with a 'monumental' production of the tragedy for which a Berlin circus was converted into an approximation of a Greek theatre; but none of this can mitigate judgment on the hybrid, highly questionable result of Hofmannsthal's operations on Sophocles.

Hofmannsthal had the ability to learn from failure as much or perhaps more than from his partial successes. The very difficulties of the task—to escape from the purely subjective, to create acting plays for the stage, not 'closet drama' for reading— stirred his imagination and so helped him to overcome the danger of stagnation which he had acknowledged in the 'Chandos Letter'. During the first decade of the new century, dramatic production gained such a hold on the poet as to become an all-absorbing preoccupation; so much so that, with a charming sense of humour, he could poke fun at his apparently haphazard choice of themes and materials when he wrote to Schnitzler: 'I want to dramatize everything that falls into my hand, even the correspondence between Schiller and Goethe, or the *Linzer Tagespost*', the dullest of provincial newspapers. Greek tragedy, adaptations of plays by Molière and Calderon, and of Otways' *Venice Preserved*, ballets, even a pantomime or two—all these were in a way essential steps on Hofmannsthal's road to the theatre. In retrospect it becomes clear that from every single new attempt he drew something important for his development, not merely in technical equipment but above all in greater understanding for the requirements of the stage and of his own potentialities.

By adapting these great classics of the world theatre, Hofmannsthal had hoped to discover the secret of the timelessness of their success; what he did learn in fact was just how far he still was from what he aimed at, from what he could do and what would satisfy him. He had to realise that with Sophocles and Otway he had once again not arrived at the real stage.

Hofmannsthal did not, fortunately, blame 'the coarse world of the theatre' for his failure to make an impression on the average theatre-goer; he sought the cause in the shortcomings of his own approach.

The desire to create for himself an audience was at the same time the recognition of the need for the creative listener, the active participant spectator. With his eyes always open for that which can draw present strength from tradition, Hofmannsthal came to consider the stage as 'the only one among the great secular institutions that had retained universal validity' and one still capable of being a true centre of festive social occasion, bringing 'art' and 'life' together. The theatre, which takes its spell from the involvement of many senses, at its best enchants and beguiles the spectator and thus makes him open and willing to be excited, to laugh and to cry, to be moved by joy or anger, to applaud or be scandalised, to identify himself with experience outside his own daily life. 'In the older world which we call medieval, but which in the form of the baroque lasted to the dawn of the nineteenth century, indeed into our own youth', Hofmannsthal wrote in one of his essays, 'everything was *spectacle:* the wedding of the feudal lord and the execution of the criminal, the reception of foreign ambassadors and the annual kermess in the village.' In all these, no less than in the 'trionfo' of the Italian cities with its pomp and circumstance, in German and Italian operas and operettas, in village melodramas and mummeries, in the passion plays, mysteries and moralities still surviving, here and there, in Austria, Bavaria and other Catholic countries, in all these he saw a living expression of the natural delight in spectacle and pageantry innate in the human race.

Out of this conception grew Hofmannsthal's hope for a renaissance of the German theatre on the foundation of a living Austrian and Bavarian baroque tradition which eventually led to the idea of the Salzburg Festival and to his own ambitious allegorical spectacles *Jedermann* and *Das grosse Salzburger Welttheater*. But the same premise, that in the theatre a state of spontaneous receptivity and participation can be created by an author who succeeds in amusing, entertaining and thus 'holding' an audience, led Hofmannsthal also in quite a different direction, to his comedies for stage and opera, especially to his social comedy *Der Schwierige*.

Hofmannsthal's comedy was not a mere funny play; his was the old conception of the term: a serious play dealing in an amusing way with a serious question. He possessed, as it proved, a very fertile dramatic imagination and often, though not invariably, succeeded in fitting his comedies, both for the dramatic and the operatic stage, with good acting plots and situations. For all that it was rarely the story which had his first concern; the true purpose of all his comedies, as indeed of all his dramatic work and of his novel, was not so much to convince the audience of the reality of the action as to open their minds to the symbolic content of the inter-relation between the figures, to that which is universally significant in individual destiny. Thus the theatre's power of magical make-believe and realisation is always directed to something which transcends the action on the stage: in *Cristinas Heimreise, Der Rosenkavalier, Arabella* to the beauty and ultimate sadness of love, resignation and acceptance; in *Ariadne auf Naxos* and *Der Schwierige* to man's isolation and to his need for loyalty and union.

Dramatic action tends to show the inter-relation and inter-dependence of human beings, the relations among individuals and their relation to the social world in which they live. 'It is the greatest gift in dramatic creation', Hofmannsthal once wrote, 'to feel the situation grow out of the very heart of the characters'. In his plays it is often through individual idiosyncracies of speech and manner more than through what is actually said or done that the situation between the characters is established and conveyed. 'The actual creative work of the poet', we read in one of Hofmannsthal's most important letters to Strauss, 'consists in finding for each individual a distinct diction, a definite style of his own. Manner of speaking, change of tone, rise and fall of voice, by these means I can establish characteristic living figures. Thus I can convey their social relationship, even much of the indefinable something which is implied between the characters and can hardly be expressed in any more direct form'. The passage refers to *Der Rosenkavalier*, but it was not until the last but one of his purely dramatic comedies, *Der Schwierige*, that Hofmannsthal showed his full mastery in suggesting a whole way of life through subtle differentiations of language and diction.

In this comedy which looks like a society piece with a plot so slender as almost to escape definition, the problem of Karl

28

Hans Bruehl, the 'difficult man', is the difficulty of communication, the doubt in its possibility: 'I understand myself much less well when I speak than when I am silent'—a situation which almost prevents him, 'reticent out of delicacy', from winning the woman he loves. In this, the most polished and successful of his plays, Hofmannsthal undoubtedly intended to commemorate a passing civilisation as *Der Rosenkavalier* had celebrated the age of Maria Theresa. In *Der Schwierige* it is the aristocratic Viennese society with all its grace and refinement of manners, tact and taste, at the moment it vanished for ever. But there is a graver, more urgent note in *Der Schwierige,* for here the author suggests, with all his affection and loyalty for a world which he knows to be doomed, the causes of its downfall; there is a parallel, more than symbolic, between the decay of society and the decay of language as a means of communication. 'The word of the common language which should hold all together', Hofmannsthal wrote almost at the same time in his Beethoven Centenary Address of 1920, 'keeps all a thousandfold apart'. Speech as an element of social intercourse, as social action *par excellence,* has become practically meaningless since there is no agreement on premises. 'Nobody knows any longer what conversation is: to give the cue to others, not to perorate oneself like a waterfall!' exclaims the host at the *soirée* in *Der Schwierige,* and we feel that he is writing *'Finis'* under a whole epoch. Here begins the Brave New World of loudspeakers, slogans and mass-propaganda.

It was Hofmannsthal's purpose 'to give the cue to others', not to preach to them but, with lightness of touch, to lead them to clearer understanding and so enable them to face the conflicts within themselves; not to use 'words which reduce all reality to the same shallow level, and smooth it over in a cloud of chatter', but to look beneath the surface matter and grasp the underlying spiritual meaning of ourselves and the universe. In the theatre he hoped to draw the audience out of themselves into a world of the imagination where he might obtain their co-operation, their active participation in the recovery of lost coherence and balance, of the missing spiritual centre.

'Let us never forget that the stage is nothing, and worse than nothing, unless it is wonderful; unless it is the dream of dreams', he said. In this attempt to use the illusion of the stage to gain a larger reality, Hofmannsthal was willing to avail himself of every means which might enable him to 'overcome the ordinary relation between spectator and actor and to free them both as much as possible; the one as host and centre, the other as active participant sharing the feast'. And if the dramatic stage, the combination of the language of words with the language of the body, the actor's miming, was not enough, he was ready to call in the aid of music, that 'language above language'. It is this which, with absolute consistency of purpose, led Hofmannsthal to opera, 'theatre plus music' as he called it himself, the addition of music to the ritual of make-believe.

IV

Hofmannsthal's work as a librettist is the story of his collaboration with Richard Strauss; it lasted, with one prolonged interruption, from the year 1906 right up to the end of the poet's life, and led to the making of six operas which have become classics of the world stage.

Publication of the correspondence between poet and composer over this period of almost 25 years has opened the workshop in which the two great artists endeavoured to create congruity out of heterogeneous material. It was a true 'working-together', a constant exchange of fertilising ideas to serve only one purpose: that 'for once music and poetry should move truly hand in hand'. Seldom have the problems and possibilities of collaboration between poet and musician been discussed with such serious and searching intensity as they are in these letters.

Hofmannsthal was not a born librettist. Characterisation based on sympathetic insight was indeed his gift, but his thought required space for its unfolding, the more so since, throughout his life, he was preoccupied with the problem of communication and beset by the horror of being misunderstood. Despite his striving for the compression and simplification which he recognised and accepted as necessary, he did not, in any of the texts which he prepared for Strauss, achieve that perfect economy of exposition, that conciseness and simplicity of execution which are regarded as essential qualities of a good libretto. Nor was his dramatic instinct invariably infallible throughout. There are a number of occasions in the correspondence with Strauss when the composer complained that the structure of certain passages or scenes 'flags, hangs fire and lacks real dramatic tension', and even took the initiative in proposing alterations and concentration, sometimes of a radical kind.

For all that, Hofmannsthal possessed an astonishing grasp of the strange medium which, though very decidely a non-musician, he had deliberately adopted; his sense for the distinctive possibilities of opera as against other art forms was striking. Late in life, in conversation with his friend Brecht, he asked himself the question: 'Why is opera my medium of expression?' 'In opera', that was his own answer, 'I can present the "significant", that which really matters, the essence, not through a process of propositions, but can take it immediately from purely emotional, more profound regions'.

The letters exchanged with the more robust and impulsive, even materialistic Strauss reveal Hofmannsthal's endeavour to fuse in opera limpid dramatic action with an awareness of the inherent complexity and tragedy of human existence. 'All the open secrets of life', he wrote to his collaborator while at work on *Ariadne auf Naxos*, 'all the secrets which we cannot bring closer than close to ourselves with words: through sound they can be drawn into our hearts, and it is to do just this that poetry calls in music'; and indeed the artistic satisfaction and lasting attraction of the Strauss-Hofmannsthal operas is due to the fact that they are at the same time sensuously appealing and emotionally moving. In contrast to so many operas of the classic repertoire, the story never falls short of the music in subtlety of thought and emotional content; what is thus achieved through the fusion of the two is a range of communication and a vitality exceeding in many respects that which word or music alone can command.

Hofmannsthal soon learnt that opera is something very different from words plus music. Right from the beginning, after the poet had suggested that he could envisage a certain sequence in *Elektra* far more powerful with music than in the original stage version, Strauss warned him: 'You expect from the music a far more powerful outward effect than it can yield in present conditions'. Hofmannsthal's reply is characteristic: 'Rest assured that I shall rely upon myself alone and not at all upon the music; this is indeed the only way in which we can and shall work together. Only this: your music will add something most beautiful, something far exceeding what the actors and the designer can ever give me'. But if the music did in fact bring this heightening and intensification of the dramatic action, Hofmannsthal had to discover the unhappy truth that in opera the music invariably tends to drown the word, so that the audience remains more or less ignorant of the details and most of the finer points of the libretto. Again and again, this 'annihilation' of the words,

31

and the problem how to make the text plain to the listener and the orchestral writing transparent, occurs as a subject of prolonged discussion in the correspondence; as was to be expected, nothing much came of this, barring a few unsatisfactory makeshift devices.

In any case, Hofmannsthal appears to have gradually realised that, although clear enunciation on the part of the singers is highly desirable to enable opera-goers to follow the words, what matters in the end is the degree to which the poet manages to convey his meaning *to the composer* and to make it understood by him. Homogeneity proved easiest to achieve where the librettist was able to build up, as in *Der Rosenkavalier* with Vienna under Maria Theresa (and again in *Arabella* for a later period), a complete and tangible, half-real, half-imaginary city world with its bustle and animation, from the levée in the palace to the backstairs world of the lackeys and to the farm-yard. Here the composer's imagination can be kindled by the living interplay and contrast between the characters of the action: the police constable and the inn-keeper, the naive bride and the two Italian conspirators, the nouveau-riche climber and the great Lady. The juxtaposition of the polished manners of young Octavian, the Rosenkavalier, and the Falstaffian character of Ochs von Lerchenau would help him, as in the famous 'Mit mir' waltz, to find characteristic musical expression for the gross, boorish proceedings and the amorous adventures of the seedy country squire; Octavian, disguised as chamber-maid, was bound to rouse the composer's sense of humour (just as Zdenka does in her innocent deceit of her sister's lover in *Arabella*); while the presentation of the silver rose, so perfectly invented, would give us Sophie's voice soaring up in ecstasy.

The opera is subtle as well as broad and comic. Indeed, even over *Der Rosenkavalier,* Strauss was anxious lest the story might prove 'too fine for the general public', and Hofmannsthal had to re-assure him: 'A pompous, fat and elderly suitor, favoured by the father, has his nose put out of joint by a dashing young lover—could anything be plainer?' The Marschallin herself, the most subtly conceived figure, has literally only a fraction of the words to speak and sing which Hofmannsthal devoted to the task of explaining to Strauss her central importance in the opera. In the end, the passionate clinging to youth which makes her stop the clocks at night-time, her lament at the passing of time in the Mirror aria:

But how can that truly be
That once I was the little Resi
And one day I too shall be an old woman
The old woman, the aged Marschallin

and the final trio where the Marschallin acts out with noble
composure her decision to resign her love:

Light one must be
With a light heart and light hands
Take and hold, hold and let go . . .

inspired some of the most moving music Strauss ever wrote.
Thus the scene transcends the gay Viennese world of Maria
Theresa and, as the little black boy trips lightly off the stage,
the final, unforgettable picture of an enchanted and enchanting
past becomes symbolic of the inevitable evanescence of every
moment of rich perfection.

The Strauss-Hofmannsthal operas (with the exception
perhaps of *Die Frau ohne Schatten,* where the poet moved in
a rarified atmosphere to which the composer could not follow
him) in performance unfold quite unmistakeably, each in
its own way, through a direct appeal to the emotions, the
significant meaning and intent which Hofmannsthal wished
them to carry. It is neither the words nor the music alone but
an idiom gained out of the conjunction of the two which lends
them conviction. No less than *Der Rosenkavalier, Ariadne
auf Naxos* and *Die ägyptische Helena* reveal Hofmannsthal's
preoccupation with time and its passing. Both operas may be
said to centre on the antithesis between transience and eternity,
between being and becoming, between permanence and mutation. In *Die ägyptische Helena* the music helps to express,
and distinguish, the two-level structure of the libretto, the
subjective spiritual action which develops parallel with the
outward events. Thus the opera suggests the working of con-
flicting symbolic forces greater than the characters themselves:
the daemonic element in Helena and the human, moral one of
Menelaos. In *Ariadne auf Naxos,* the attempt to open up the
circumscribed stage to the world at large and 'to extend it into
the infinite' led Hofmannsthal, as elsewhere on occasion, to
mythology and the supernatural. Here the main action is raised
out of the realm of ordinary existence into the sphere of the
gods, and since the music helps further to suspend the critical
faculties, the audience is led immediately into a world of the

33

imagination where spiritual experience of a higher order becomes communicable, and its universal validity acceptable.

In this way *Ariadne auf Naxos,* prepared, as the author himself chose to pretend, 'merely as a wire frame on which to hang the music prettily', is in fact perhaps the most delicately wrought of the six operas for, behind the gay fable of the old story, attention is focussed on a deeper meaning: the glory of the steadfast heart. Even the seemingly fortuitous linking up of the *Vorspiel* (with the parvenu's scheme for simultaneous performance of the love story of Ariadne and the buffo farce of the faithless Zerbinetta), and the opera itself as a play within the play, this odd combination turns out to be one of the poet's happiest ideas. In the person of the central figure, the young composer, we experience Eros in his double-faced, dual aspect; heavenly and all too earthly love, reconciled in a hymnic close of music.

In a letter written after a temporary disagreement, Hofmannsthal told Strauss: 'For us to be rent asunder, or not-to-come-together, that would be a major disaster, a festering wound, or even a permanent crippling of our joint child. That would prove correct those friends and strangers who incessantly, by letter and by word of mouth, directly and indirectly, tell me or get others to tell me, write to me or get others to write to me that I ought to abandon this collaboration. I prefer to take my own counsel which assures me that together we may yet achieve something valuable at least now and then; perhaps even produce something universally significant by creating a flawless work of art, truly satisfying and in every way harmonious.'

With his willing devotion to the task in hand, Hofmannsthal proved over and over again that it is possible and worth while to write opera libretti of high literary quality and real distinction. Strauss, in turn, aware of his good fortune, recognised the libretti which his collaborator offered him as works of art in their own right, and he respected them as such. Yet there was a give-and-take in this workshop which made it possible for composer and poet alike never to feel unduly fettered; both realised that out of words and music a new unit was to be forged. It was Hofmannsthal who, in a postscript, spoke of the work when it was done:

'He who separates here will do harm. He who seeks to single out one aspect forgets that, unknowing, he strikes the chords of the whole. The music must not be torn from the words, the words not from the living dramatic picture . . . A work of art is one whole, and even two men's work can be one whole.'

34

V

Hofmannsthal once quoted the following passage from Lucian's περὶ ὀρχήσεως: 'When every spectator becomes one with what happens on the stage, when everyone recognises in the performance, as in a mirror, the reflection of his own true impulses, then, but not until then, success has been achieved. Such a dumb spectacle is at the same time nothing less than the fulfilment of the Delphic maxim 'Know thyself', and those who return from the theatre have experienced what was truly an experience.' With his adaptations from Sophocles, Hofmannsthal had discovered that Greek tragedy, owing to its specific conventions and limitations, can no longer create such a direct collective experience for a modern audience. In *Jedermann* and *Das grosse Salzburger Welttheater,* still trying to base himself on a form of dramatic representation earlier than the modern 'literary' theatre, he turned with far greater success to the medieval western tradition of the allegorical religious spectacle.

Jedermann, begun in 1904 but not completed and performed until 1911, is derived from the English morality *Everyman.* Sir George Franckenstein, after seeing a performance in London, had drawn Hofmannsthal's attention to the old play, and the poet himself likens his own work to a mere 'cleaning off the cobwebs from an old clockwork so that with the chiming of the hours the old figures will appear again'. The sequence of events in Everyman's citation before the Lord as he is divested, step by step, of all his possessions, his desertion by his friends, his penitence and redemption by Good Works and Faith, all this follows closely the morality play; only the banqueting scene which adds colour to the spectacle (suggested by Max Reinhardt) and the cheated devil are major (and well fitting) original introductions. Nor did Hofmannsthal in any way attempt to individualise the characters. Everyman as well as the minor human figures which appear in this Dance of Death are representative types; indeed it would seem that what attracted the poet to the old morality with its timeless truth was the very fact that man in general, that each member of the audience, is, so to speak, himself on the stage: *Sua res agitur.* The essay 'Das alte Spiel vom Jedermann' (1912) shows that Hofmannsthal was above all concerned that his play be taken by a simple, naive audience as an unfolding of essential Christian truths and moral attitudes, and—whether he succeeded as fully as he believed, and whether or not the magnificent setting on the

35

Salzburg Domplatz, where *Jedermann* is usually performed, actually gave him, as he believed, 'a crowd of spectators where the gap between the educated and the people has disappeared'— it is perhaps not permissible to judge such an attempt by literary standards alone. Impressive though the spectacle is, it makes one wonder whether it might not have gained if performed as a dumb show. To some extent this may be due to the language of the play; all the figures speak in exactly the same rather self-conscious idiom which is largely modelled on the homely *Knüppelreim* of Hans Sachs, the Nuremberg shoemaker-cum-poet, but strikes one in fact as 'antique', a second-hand language with a period flavour not very happily resurrected. The figures, moreover, declaim each for himself, not so much addressing each other as the spectator—a feature no doubt to some extent inherent in a representation in which we are all on the stage, but one which tends to give the later part of this 'human fairy tale in Christian dress' more and more the aspect of a sermon.

The message of *Jedermann* is that this life is part of a greater life; that the world is but a passing stage, and that, for our actions on it, we shall all be called to account on the Day of Judgement. When Hofmannsthal returned to allegory some ten years later with *Das grosse Salzburger Welttheater* (1922), God, 'the Master', actually tells a personified World to stage this life as a play. This metaphor of human life as a spectacle played out before the eyes of God is taken from Calderon's *Great Theatre of the World*. Here and elsewhere, the great Catholic playwright's baroque drama, centred not on human beings and psychological conflicts but on the relation between man and God, between divine grace and human freedom, offered the Austrian poet a model and inspiration for his own endeavour to encompass in one personal vision the whole of the universe, the 'imperishable timeless root of things'. From Calderon also comes the conception which presents the souls dressed—and stripped again—before our eyes with the parts allotted to them: Beauty and Wisdom, King, Rich Man, Peasant, Beggar. The fading and leavetaking of these six allegorical figures is an impressive device which shows visually, in the most direct way in which such truth can be brought home to an audience, the fleeting nature of life, the theme of the spectacle itself. Yet, for all this affinity with Calderon, Hofmannsthal claimed *Das grosse Salzburger Welttheater* as his own, and rightly so, because the powerful *active* figure of the beggar here

36

gives the play an entirely new dramatic meaning and climax.

The beggar, who stands for the have-nots who demand to have, for the lawless as well as those who enjoy no rights, for the oppressed as well as those who are in constant revolt, this beggar is yet a highly individualised figure, facing, for one dramatic moment, the whole world. When, in his wrath, he raises the axe to strike and bring down not merely established order, King, Rich Man, Peasant, but also Beauty and Wisdom and Piety, we know that this is the threat of chaos against the very idea of order; we realise at once that if the beggar does strike he will destroy all. Yet by a lightning illumination he is inspired to lay the axe aside, and the play can go on.

The figure of the beggar points, in a manner perhaps more powerful than the profane theatre can often achieve, the antithesis between man's destructive instinct and the creative power of moral decision. Man is not dependent on circumstances, not a blind object but, under the eye of God, master of his destiny in a constant shouldering, a taking-upon-himself of decision: 'So that he may take his choice, I have granted man the spark of supreme freedom', says the Master. The infinite forbearance of the Lord imposes upon man ultimate God-like responsibility; by his non-action 'the beggar has done the decisive deed of his life'. All is in the moral choice.

There is no doubt that Hofmannsthal intended to present *Das grosse Salzburger Welttheater* as a parable for our time. It is certain that he saw the ghost of Bolshevism plainly behind the words and gestures of the beggar. Through this figure he re-affirmed in the troubled years immediately after the world war his faith in man, his certainty that it depends on the individual alone, on his free decision, whether crises and catastrophies, personal and collective, will lead to utter ruin or, despite everything, forward to a new future. It strikes one therefore all the more as an unfortunate weakness of *Das grosse Salzburger Welttheater* that the motivation of the beggar's momentous change of mind (the μετανοεῖν) is not altogether convincing. We ask ourselves: is it love that suddenly touches him? is it a miracle? a dream, a mystical experience, or a deliberate about-face? Is he afraid of his own power or indifferent to it? We only see him as he abruptly turns his back on this world and disappears into the wood, a hermit and saint. When it was suggested to Hofmannsthal that there was a lack of consistency in the beggar's part, he seems to have thought that 'this unusual medium' (of the allegorical play), 'will not, any more than

in *Jedermann,* allow the central figure and its symbolic experience to be taken for truly personal, individual experience'. The
answer was plainly not altogether satisfactory even to him.
During the remaining years of his life (switching from allegory
to a more realistic, historical drama) Hofmannsthal wrestled
in *Der Turm* with the problem how to convey his faith in this
inner freedom of man, in 'something higher which stands above
the power struggle of this earth'.

VI

Hofmannsthal's work in narrative prose is not voluminous.
Apart from fragments which may still be in the hands of his
literary executors awaiting publication, all we have are three
'Novellen': *Reitergeschichte* (1898), *Bassompierre* (1900) and
Lucidor (1910); and four other stories, best described as fairy
tales, of which two, *Märchen der 672. Nacht* and *Die Frau
ohne Schatten* were completed. Hofmannsthal made only one
attempt in the direction of the novel, to which he gave the
provisional title *Andreas oder Die Vereinigten.* Its abandonment
after about one quarter of the projected length was written
implied that no more was to be done in this genre.

As it is, the *Andreas* fragment, just over one hundred pages,
contains some of Hofmannsthal's finest prose, pure, crystal
clear classic German, the language of Goethe and Stifter, un-
equalled and even unapproached by any of his contemporaries.
Here the poet succeeded in combining great depth of thought
and rich imagery with complete simplicity of language, and the
effortlessness of the whole makes this, even in its fragmentary
state, one of the most enchanting things he has written.

The subject of the novel was described by Hofmannsthal
himself in a letter to Richard Strauss (in 1914) as 'die Entwick-
lung eines jungen Wieners zum Menschen'—how a young Viennese
comes to reach manhood. It is the story of a young Viennese
gentleman of good family, named Andreas von Ferschengelder,
who is sent by his parents to Venice to finish and broaden his
education, and of his adventures on this journey into life. The
conception was that of the great *Bildungsroman,* of which
the outstanding example in German literature is Goethe's
Wilhelm Meister, and, when one remembers the fate of Novalis'
Ofterdingen, it is perhaps not altogether surprising that it
failed to reach completion.

The period in which the action is laid is the time of the
Empress Maria Theresa and, given the fact that the poet carried
in him the blood of Austrian peasants on the one side and that
of a Lombard patrician family on the other, his choice of setting,
a mountain farm in Carinthia and the city of Venice in her
decline, gains special significance. The story opens one night
in September 1778, with Andreas stranded, his luggage beside
him, on the stone steps leading up from one of the countless
minor canals of this mysterious city. Hardly is the young man
installed in lodgings when, by a flash-back of his memory, we
are transported to the mountains of Carinthia and to the humili-
ating experience which befell him there. This long chapter
brings Andreas and his servant, in search of shelter, to an ancient fortified manor, the Finazzerhof, more castle than farm-
house, tucked away in the Carinthian Alps, and describes
his meeting there with Romana, the farmer's daughter. The
three days which follow are full of richly contrasting moods
and incident. The nascent, child-like love between the two young
people is enfolded, embedded in the deep peace of the alpine
landscape and the ageless routine of country activities: the
clattering of the horses' hoofs on the flagstones of the farm-yard,
the goats crowding round the milking-pail, the puddle with the
quacking ducks, the fine big cock on the dung-heap. Against
this pastoral idyll is set the insolent, lewd depravity of the
servant Gotthilff who has forced himself on the irresolute
Andreas somewhere along the road and now mocks him, making
free with a dairymaid in the stable. At night, Andreas is woken
out of heavy uneasy sleep by frightful screams only to find the
servant girl, tied half naked to a smouldering bed-post, a gag
on the floor beside her and the room ablaze, while the fiendish
ruffian, of course, has long made his escape, helping himself to
his master's horse and the travel-money sown into the saddlebag.

Thus the young man's joy in his new-found love is grimly
marred by the shame and horror which he has brought on his
host's household; such is his sense of inadequacy that, though he
can feel in the nearness of the beloved the promise of paradise,
she is to him unreachable. The parting is inevitable: Andreas
cannot possess Romana until he has learnt to believe in himself
and so to believe in her and in the possibility of their union.
One of the finest passages in a chapter full of unforgettable
scenes is that of the barefooted Romana, her mouth struggling
with words, her eyes with tears at the pain of his departure,
tearing from her neck a narrow silver chain and pressing it on

39

the back of Andreas' hand so hard that he has to pick up the broken pieces. And again Andreas' journey from the Finazzer farm late in the afternoon: the long shadows falling into the deep valley and on the winding stream below, the larch forests, blue-black masses clinging to the riven slopes of the mountain, the waterfall plunging into the ravine, and upwards the bare mountain boldly rising, inclines of sheer naked rock, crowned at last by the glistening snowbound peak, pristine and brilliant, an eagle circling high up in the pure evening air—'it came to him that seen from high above, the parted are united and the sense of loneliness and isolation is an illusion. He possessed Romana wherever he was, he was carrying her with him wherever he might go . . . An unutterable assurance befell him; it was the happiest moment of his life.'

This sudden flash of insight, this momentary illumination, is in a way an anticipation of the end of the novel such as Hofmannsthal must have envisaged it; but it is only through experience that Andreas can gain lasting certainty of that which was here vouchsafed him in a moment of exaltation. Before he can be united to Romana he must become a man. Thus the journey into life is also a journey towards her. Of this journey, the finished fragment such as we have it contains apparently little more than the exposition: the picture of Andreas as an adolescent, as a young man at the outset of the search for himself. On careful reading of the text, however, and of the voluminous notes and jottings for the continuation which Hofmannsthal left, it becomes evident that the poet had already so fully penetrated and mastered his subject matter that the description he gives of the adolescent Andreas carries with it, by implication, the prospect of Andreas as a mature man.

With the same strength of character and moral courage which had enabled him to reject the temptation to build a protective shell around himself, and to accept instead the disappointments, the pain and suffering of laying himself open to the world, Hofmannsthal, by creating Andreas, now faced in retrospect every aspect of his own adolescence to show the way to true maturity. Andreas is a most lovable young man, highly sensitive, and profoundly unsure of himself and of his capacity to come to terms with life. Like the child-like Parsifal, he does not dare to ask; when addressed by others, his first reaction is: 'This man cannot be much good, since he has time to waste on me'. Uncertainty and timidity prevent him from taking any decision or from committing himself to any resolution once taken:

'What kind of man would I have to be', he asks himself at a vital juncture 'to take this upon myself and then to stand my ground?' The hero's naivety is sometimes comic even to his creator: 'Andreas suddenly blushed so furiously that a haze blurred his eyes, and he nearly slipped on a squashed tomato lying in his way.' Everything happens to him as to one who is a puppet in the hands of circumstance: he suffers the impudent Gotthilff to force his detested services upon him and allows him to brag of lewd adventures which drive the blood to his cheek; he always wishes to be where he is not or leaves where he would give his life to remain. At one point during his stay at the Finazzerhof he attempts to run away even from himself: 'He measured the bounds so that with each he was hidden behind massive tree-trunks: there were old maples and beeches still standing among the pines and he hid behind them, then bounded on until he had escaped from himself as from a prison.'

In Andreas' childhood memories 'there is always something painfully confusing which his whole life will hardly suffice (so it appears to him) to unravel'. In one of his childish dreams which keep coming back to him he had crept hungry to the pantry to cut himself a piece of bread; there he stood, knife in hand, pressing the loaf to his body but cutting, again and again, past the loaf into the void. In another dream Andreas hears Romana screaming for help; to reach her, he must squeeze himself through a wardrobe full of his parents' clothes. 'There were too many worn-out clothes, the clothes of many years which had not been given away. Dripping with sweat he pushed his way through.' A note for a conversation between Andreas and his mentor, the Maltese Knight, contains the answer: 'Only he holds the past in dread who, remaining at an inferior stage, imagines that it might all have turned out otherwise.'

Much of this penetrating analysis of adolescent bewilderment, quoted here from Hofmannsthal's notes for *Andreas,* is still in the form of abstract reflections; the few chapters which the author carried out fully show that all these reflections were to be translated, like the dream of the wardrobe and the flight through the forest, into visual experience. All Hofmannsthal's narrative work aimed at this: consciously avoiding expression of ideas in abstract propositions, he always attempted to communicate them directly to the senses, particularly, since his was predominantly a visual rather than an aural imagination, to make them visual as concrete incidents and experiences.

41

Necessarily, to convey the full range of his ideas and reflections he needed striking images and incidents. In all his prose, the more phantastic or enigmatic the action or phenomenon he intended to relate, the more tangible, detailed and precise was his description of the minute particulars making up the whole. 'The most wonderful poetic sentences', Hofmannsthal once wrote, 'are those which present with great physical precision something physically impossible; they are true creations through the word.' So strange indeed are some of the situations in *Andreas* that the utmost perfection of this art was required to make them appear as natural as they do. The first person whom Andreas meets in Venice, a courteous gentleman who shows him the way, turns out to be entirely naked under his cloak, barring a shirt; next day Andreas learns of a lottery whose sole prize is the virginity of the daughter of a Venetian count; and during a visit to a celebrated beauty he encounters another nobleman who, in a fit of jealousy, swallows his mistress' cage bird.

Most strange of all, but possessing a symbolic meaning not difficult to penetrate, is the double figure of Maria-Mariquita. Andreas notices Maria first as he enters a church and sees her in the semi-darkness kneeling at a *prie-dieu* near the altar, a woman oppressed by sickness either of body or of mind, seeking relief from suffering in prayer; but hardly has he stepped out again onto the sunlit piazza than Mariquita slips out of the church behind him and, with the audacity of the experienced courtesan, brushes past him with curls flying that nearly touch his cheek, so swiftly and so close that he feels the air stirred. A few minutes later, he steps into the courtyard of a house and there a young girl—Maria or Mariquita?—her body outstretched on the light trellis of the roof, reaches out towards him through the golden vine-leaves and the rich ripe grapes as if to stroke his head, and disappears.

These situations and incidents, highly daring and completely successful, could hardly be made natural and convincing except in a setting such as is offered to the author by the Venice of Francesco Guardi with its incessant, nervous, restless movement, with the lapping of the waves against the walls of crumbling palaces, the darting high-lights and the deep-black shadows. In this charmed, bewitched bazaar among its maze of alleys and canals, its constant flow of adventurers and lovers, of masks and impossible fancy-dress figures, the young Andreas gradually, through intrigues and entanglements, delight and disappointments, temptation and revelation, through guilt and mistake, sudden insight and periods of utter confusion finds the road to his true self, to maturity. Here again it is the choice of Venice, vanity fair in its decay, which enables Hofmannsthal to make his purpose unobtrusively clear: Venice teaches Andreas, and through him the reader, the vanity of the way of the world: here it is impossible to take appearances at their face value; everything leads to the search for the reality behind them.

Andreas begins to see that all equilibrium in life must 'rest on healthy self-confidence and assurance'; this and much else of the utmost importance to his development towards maturity he was to learn, according to Hofmannsthal's plan, in encounter and in conversation with his spiritual teacher, the Maltese Knight Sacramozo. Unfortunately we have little more than the outline of this important figure (in whom it is perhaps permissible to discern one aspect of the author himself). By the time he abandoned his novel, Hofmannsthal had jotted down a large number of ideas for Sacramozo's character and above all for Andreas' conversation with him, without, however, as yet turning them into the graphic incidents he undoubtedly had in mind. These notes, highly suggestive like many of Hofmannsthal's drafts which remained fragmentary—among them the intriguing 'Brief des letzten Contarin'—are so rich and revealing that one feels impelled to follow them further and perceive in them a statement of what Hofmannsthal considered essential steps towards individual maturity, a statement which throws much light on all his work.

'Andreas' path', so runs one of the notes, *'first to become capable of love,* then to learn that body and spirit are one'. What is love? Understanding for the needs of others, consideration, attention; 'attention', says Sacramozo, 'attention means as much as love. I ask you to treat my soul with attention. Who is attentive? The diplomat, the official, the doctor, the priest . . . not one of them attentive enough. The statement "I have neglected nothing"—who can pronounce it of himself with full conviction?' Closely connected with this is a passage from Hofmannsthal's essay on Goethe's *West-Oestlicher Divan*: 'The bizarre fascinates the eye, the exaggerated forces itself upon the mind, even emptiness and ugliness have their appeal: yet to perceive that which is pure and strong calls for attentiveness. Thus it is among men: can we take in the best and purest others have to give, unless we are raised to a state of mind which we call love? . . . How rare is a sensitive eye, an attentive ear, an open heart!' Again: 'We live truly but in the eyes of those who love us'; and conversely, says Sacramozo: 'To that which we can fully share, we are already half united'.

'Andreas' path: first to become capable of love, then *to learn that body and spirit are one*. He has suffered constantly from this dualism; now the one, now the other seems worthless to him. At last he learns to feel the one behind the other, to feel that the one always sustains the other.' The double figure, Maria-Mariquita, outward projection of this rift in Andreas' personality, of the conflict between his spiritual aspirations and his physical desires, and yet a living human being, is Hofmannsthal's brilliant device and symbol to unfold this profound lesson in maturity. Day after day, Andreas recoils from the physical attraction which Mariquita offers him and seeks safety in the purity, the religious aestheticism of Maria, only to be driven back to the other. 'Andreas', so runs a passage in the notes to the novel, 'with all his nature needed and longed for passion which, by carrying us away, releases us of the burden of self.' Yet he shrinks from relinquishing his hold upon himself and maintains his uniqueness with that obstinate clinging to innocence which Claudio in *Der Tor und der Tod* (who has many traits in common with the immature Andreas) overcomes only too late. So Andreas, at the outset of the novel, cannot think of women except to wish 'it were all over, that he were older and had children of his own . . . and that the world was clean and kindly like a Sunday morning with the bells ringing'.

Addison's 'the whole man must move at once' was a favourite quotation of Hofmannsthal's: Andreas has still to understand that both Maria *and* Mariquita offer him what he needs; that the one and the other are mere segments of human personality which he must join together. Coming from the North, he must learn in life that which is innate wisdom of the Latin races: the knowledge of the essential unity, for good *and* evil, of body and spirit. Only when he has accomplished this will he understand how the girl Romana, in all her crystal-clear innocence, can give herself to him 'so lightly and so whole-heartedly'. Only then can he possess her, for he will believe in her and know her as one complete, mature human being can know another.

It may well be that, in his attempt to display man in his fulness, the figure of Andreas such as he had hoped to draw him raised questions which eventually eluded the poet's own grasp. Here in the endeavour to reach and understand himself he may have come upon problems unsolved and insoluble in his own personality, too close and too intricate to allow of that 'taking distance' which the artist requires to impose shape upon his creatures. Perhaps this is what Broch has attempted to indicate when he used the inelegant phrase that the novel or its continuance 'was incompatible with the poet's need for "I" suppression'.

Another, less speculative, reason is that the collapse of the traditional social structure of Europe and even, close at home, of its political forms, forced upon Hofmannsthal's attention a specific, partial aspect of the problem: the nature and ethics of man's social involvement, and these preoccupations took shape in such works as *Die Frau ohne Schatten, Das grosse Salzburger Welttheater* and, above all, in *Der Turm*.

VII

In *Andreas*, Hofmannsthal was chiefly preoccupied with the individual and his growth toward maturity, although a passing, almost centemporary comment (1915) on this work suggests that the story was perhaps also to be read on another level as a discussion of the German character in a more general way: 'If one regards the eighteenth century as the adolescence of the modern German', the poet wrote, 'it must be said that it was a dangerous adolescence: narrow, vapid, and calculated to undermine self-assurance, to create a gap between spirit and life'. It is certain that, as he grew older, and especially after the world war, Hofmannsthal was more and more driven towards an examination of the social position of man in the community, until, in his final work, *Der Turm*, the individual, as ζῷον πολιτικον, is placed almost exclusively, if in a highly individual way, in the hub of public life.

Die Frau ohne Schatten (completed as a libretto in 1915 but not performed until 1919) may be regarded as the connecting link between *Andreas* and *Der Turm*. The story, in its oriental fairyland setting, turns once more on the search for the road to true humanity, but the test of human action appears firmly focussed on (if not yet, as in *Der Turm*, actually subordinated to) the needs and purposes of society as a whole. As in the comedies which the poet wrote at about this time, marriage and parenthood are conceived as the mainstay of social existence. Central to the whole fable (though by no means easy to fathom) is Hofmannsthal's interpretation of the meaning of conjugal love and of the child to be born as representing continuity.

45

In discussing *Die Frau ohne Schatten* after both the libretto and the subsequent prose version were completed, Hofmannsthal said that Goethe's

Von dem Gesetz, das alle Wesen bindet,
Befreit der Mensch sich, der sich überwindet

Through self-conquest man frees himself from the law that binds all creatures.

was the core of his story, though the couplet might well have served as a motto for many of his later works, not least *Das grosse Salzburger Welttheater* and *Der Turm*. A fairy, daughter of the Gods, who has power to assume all forms of life, falls in love with a human, the Emperor, and in marrying him takes human destiny upon herself. The Empress, who is thus part animal, part woman, part spirit, has to acquire a shadow as symbol and sign of her acceptance of man's creature existence; to become a full human being, she must become a mother. Although to her, as a spirit-born being, this prospect is abhorrent, her love for the Emperor (who will be turned to stone unless she bears him a child) leads her to humble herself ever deeper in sharing more and more of human life, only to realise at last that her end, fertility, can only be gained at the expense of two poor human beings, the simple-minded dyer and his beautiful wife. Faced with this choice, the 'woman without a shadow' refuses to secure her own happiness by sacrificing that of the humble couple for whom her sympathy is roused, and by this very decision she becomes truly human and is granted a shadow. The sacrifice deliberately accepted for the sake of coming generations is rewarded, the beloved is redeemed and a child is the fruit of that submission which exalts.

Into this fable of *Die Frau ohne Schatten* (which he always considered one of his most important works) Hofmannsthal poured an abundance of ideas of profound significance to him, and Strauss presented him with an outstanding score which is among the most richly inventive this composer has ever produced. Yet the fate of this extremely ambitious opera did not fulfil the high expectations poet and composer placed in it; it is but infrequently performed and has never been performed in England. The reason is that the work makes not only immense demands on producer, orchestra and voices, but possibly still higher ones on the audience.

Writing to Richard Strauss when the theme of *Die Frau ohne Schatten* first presented itself to him, Hofmannsthal suggested that 'the opera, such as it has taken shape in my mind, might stand in much the same relation to *Die Zauberflöte* as our *Rosenkavalier* does to *Figaro*'.

Unfortunately, aware that no later work could hope to match Mozart's opera in ingenuous charm and simplicity, the poet —always inclined to over-elaboration—here pressed the spiritual conflict to a point of subtlety and his metaphoric meaning to a point of intricacy where Strauss' music could no longer help to sustain the plot and carry it forward, but on the contrary inevitably had to drown it. Thus the opera has come to be likened not unfairly to a gorgeous barge over-weighted with symbols and too cumbersome to move. Here the limits of romantic opera were not only reached but strained, and even Hofmannsthal himself came to realise this eventually when he wrote to his collaborator: 'In *Die Frau ohne Schatten* we have lacked lightness of touch.'

That Strauss is hardly to be blamed for this result seems to be demonstrated by what happened later to the libretto. Engrossed in his subject and its implications, Hofmannsthal proceeded to re-write the story in prose—'the most difficult task', he confessed at the time, 'I have ever undertaken'. *Die Frau ohne Schatten* as a poetic fairy tale, the only major prose work which Hofmannsthal completed, was intended to exemplify the Novalis epigram he was fond of quoting: 'The impossible is the true realm of poetry.' There are indeed passages of great beauty in this ambitious long story where Hofmannsthal does succeed, as in *Andreas,* in divesting the magic of its improbability, and reaches solidity and relief of action which might arouse the envy of any writer of realistic prose.

It is a far cry, even so, from the fairy tale as a deliberately adopted literary art form to the fairy story of popular tradition which Hofmannsthal believed he was here continuing and, to use another term coined by Novalis, 'revivifying'. Hofmannsthal had a firm belief in 'a mythological firmament stretching over the whole of the old Europe: names, conceptions, figures with whom a higher meaning is associated, personified forces of the moral order'. In these he expected to find a universally valid means of communication to convey what is essentially a Christian message, as in *Jedermann* and *Das grosse Salzburger Welttheater,* but a far more elaborate one.

Unfortunately, Hofmannsthal tended to overestimate—a fallacy which seems to some extent indissolubly tied up with all his efforts to recall the twentieth century to its foundations—the spontaneity with which modern consciousness responds to the evocation of its own tradition.

Now that he was freed from the restraint which the libretto had imposed upon him, Hofmannsthal wove into his gradually unfolding narrative further ideas and *motifs* which he had, no doubt reluctantly, omitted from the opera. Central among these is the scene where the unborn children offer a banquet to their father to bring home to him the duty of generation as the foremost meaning of life. Almost every other of the countless symbolic details which the poet employed—the petrification, the absence of the shadow, the red falcon, the rudderless boat, the golden stream of life, the bath of purification, the little fishes which the old nurse fries in the kitchen—belong to ancient mythology.

It may be that such intermingling of Christian ethics with pre-Christian myth and imagery was bound to confuse rather than clarify the poet's purpose. Perhaps even those who are able to follow the thread through mythology and allegory, through mysticism and philosophy, in a setting now realistic, now supernatural, may find his ultimate intention, though undoubtly high-minded, somewhat disappointing in proportion to the immense effort required. For Hofmannsthal's magic carpet, however colourful and rich the pattern, turns out so densely woven that its very iridescence bewilders the vision; the symbolism, entwined as it is to the point of mystification, can hardly deliver to the modern reader the whole message which it is meant to convey. No more than Strauss in the opera did Hofmannsthal in the fairy tale succeed in achieving that gossamer transparency which alone could have given it the life essential to his conception of *Die Frau ohne Schatten* as a popular work in an ancient medium.

VIII

At least four volumes of the collected edition of Hugo von Hofmannsthal's works now in process of publication are devoted to literary criticism, essays and addresses, prose writings which accompany the poet's creative work from early adolescence to the time of his death. A mere glance at their titles and subjects makes it obvious that here was at work one of the few minds of this century who can be called truly European. From childhood Hofmannsthal must have read widely and systematically not only the German classics but equally French, English, Italian and (to a lesser extent) the literature of Eastern countries. What makes him 'European', however, is neither the familiarity with which he moved among the great names and the great books of many nations and languages, nor his high sensitivity to that which was lasting and significant in tradition or in the contemporary trends he discussed, but the fact that to him the great works of art, of whatever period and whatever national background, all fell into place as part of the European inheritance. Whatever he touched, with seeming catholicity of taste— Shakespeare, Poe and Pater; Molière, Balzac and Victor Hugo; Calderon, Goldoni and D'Annunzio; Novalis, Stifter and Raimund—all, as he saw them, were in some way related to each other, and so to him: not isolated phenomena of the gift of genius casually scattered, but fruit from one large tree in whose shelter our world has grown.

Hofmannsthal did not create a new faith (like Stefan George) nor seek, discover and express new knowledge (like Rilke); yet throughout his work one feels a definite sense of purpose, which became increasingly a conscious one. This purpose was to counteract, in a time of progressive fragmentation, the centrifugal influences at work by recalling the binding elements of our culture, the substance on which our life is based: the living, dynamic force of western tradition. When he adapted the literary products of other ages and countries and in the process assimilated them as his own, it was to make their universality and kinship, their permanence and present relevance known again; as we see them through his eyes, pulsating with new life, they prove to be not strangers but concerned with our human situation, with our common values.

His wide knowledge of history and literature was to Hofmannsthal not an intellectual possession alone which he had to administer for his own and future generations. It was a patrimony of the heart, which, by filling it with new life and warmth, he sought to preserve from neglect and oblivion, for in the common 'waste of substance' he saw self-desertion and an impoverishment of the collective mind which must lead to chaos. It is consciousness of, and loyalty to, the tradition out of which and into which he has been born that offers man the only possible fulfilment of his desire 'to attach himself, to belong somewhere' and so to gain security, a firm foothold amid the changes of time and fortune. To succeed, he must take possession of his inheritance, and tend it.

To Hofmannsthal a force making for order and preservation appeared no less creative than one producing new things. In this spirit he adapted Molière, Otway, and Calderon for the modern stage as an invigorating return to the foundations. In this spirit he assembled his collections of the treasures of German literary tradition which he edited and introduced: *Deutsche Erzähler* (1912), an anthology of older narrative writers, published as if to remind his contemporaries, at a threatening moment in their history, of imperishable resources common to them all; *Deutsches Lesebuch* (1922/3), a collection of prose during the time of its finest flowering from 1750 to 1850; and *Wert und Ehre deutscher Sprache* (1927), twelve important discussions of the spirit of the German language for which he wrote a moving introduction expressing 'the melancholy thought' that the language of the great works of art might be 'moving towards the day when it will no longer be understood'. And during the world war, 'because at times when the ground is sliding under our foot, we can find assurance in the company of those who are secure for all times', he conceived the idea of an *Österreichische Bibliothek,* a collection of small reprints of all that is best in Austrian literature through the centuries.

It is characteristic of Hofmannsthal's conception of Austria that this series, which appeared between 1915 and 1917 in the format of the well-known Insel books and was intended 'to make the voice of Austria heard among those who love her', should have included at least one volume of Slav origin, an anthology of Czech lyrical poems in translation. Hofmannsthal has been called, in no limiting sense, 'the spiritual sublimation of the old Austria, of Austro-Hungary'. Certainly, descendant of Austrian peasant stock on his mother's side, and of a minor Italian patrician house on his father's, not without an admixture of Bohemian and Jewish blood, he carried in him the very elements which the empire attempted to combine. Whole-hearted Austrian as he was, the position of this vast political compound 'in the borderland between Roman, German, Slav', and its historic mission as he saw it, were of decisive importance in forming his character and his views.

But to him, who was rarely too close to any event or institution, imperial Austria was far more than an administrative unit; it was a social and spiritual conception reaching far beyond the confines of the clumsy apparatus of a dynastic state at pains to hold together its waning power. He saw his country more receptive than France to foreign ideas and points of view, less insular than Britain, less isolated than Spain, more human, more adaptable, less rigid than the Germans, with a balance and lightness of its own, 'acting, not according to principles, but to spontaneous, natural instincts'; a supra-national society, above all, where 'nationalism is considered not merely something limiting, but positively immoral'. Situated at the crux, the meeting point of East and West, North and South, Austria was in his eyes the natural heart of Europe, the core of the old Europe out of which a new European community (a community including the Slav nations) might grow. The grandeur as well as the peril of her thousand year old history he saw in a never-ending reconciling of tensions within, a maintenance of contact and conversation without, a fertile harmonising of conflicts and contrasts.

When August 1914 came, the war of which he was to write later: 'It is the open outbreak of a revolution which in the course of the century will deny everything we are and everything we ever possessed', the first impression was, as Jacob Wassermann has recorded, 'like the blinding of an eagle'. Yet, if it was his tragedy to see the Empire falling apart, the old loyalties broken, the very foundations of his Europe in dissolution and decay, his was not a barren, obstinate clinging to the past. Even in the middle of the war, Hofmannsthal's addresses were directed towards the building of a new future, as we can see from the notes for his '*Speeches in Scandinavia*' (the full texts of which are not preserved) with their emphasis on the need to 'gain, out of the war, a new, purer conception of freedom'; from '*Die österreichische Idee*' (1917) where a tribute to the old Empire's task of 'conciliation, synthesis, bridging of cleavage' becomes a programmatic demand for a new Europe; above all from his great address in Switzerland (1916), '*Die Idee Europa*', in which he calls for 'a new European idea, a new reality. Not Utopia, not confederation, not a permanent international congress, though all these may come—but a new European "I", a changed relation of the "I" to existence'.

This reintegration of Europe in the realm of thought was a conception both conservative and revolutionary. To Hofmannsthal, who was always aware of the perennial antagonism between man's need for hierarchy and order on the one hand and innovation on the other, between 'being' and 'becoming', who constantly strove for synthesis above the conflict, there was no irreconcil-

51

able contradiction between the two terms. His conception was conservative in its steadfast adherence to the 'treasures and liberties' secured in the past, and in its recognition of tradition as the only common ground for discussion, yet it was revolutionary in being always open and susceptible to growth and mutation.

In the search for 'a new reality which we are laboriously creating for ourselves', a Europe seen as a transcendent community, a coherent civilisation based on common adherence and joint responsibility for a great intellectual patrimony, the poet's task is unambiguous. He must communicate his knowledge of higher, universal, lasting values and make this knowledge, in Mathew Arnold's phrase, prevail.

It was in this sense that Hofmannsthal accepted his own responsibility and calling: not merely serving his time, but in the service of all times; ever conscious of the place of art in the community, not indeed supreme, but as an integral part of harmonious existence. Thus it came about that, in 1920, he was the leading spirit behind the foundation of the Salzburg Festival, as a visible demonstration, amid the devastation caused by the war, of the sustaining, conciliating qualities of art.

Even at the worst point of post-war depression, suffering himself under the privations which followed in the wake of defeat, Hofmannsthal asserted his confidence, in his '*Beethoven Address*' (1920), that 'while the nation lies prostrate . . . like a sick man, individuals still remain mindful of the higher spiritual values and of the need to overcome through them the dumb, unsociable element in the German nation'. To this problem he returned again with his powerful if difficult address, '*Das Schrifttum als geistiger Raum der Nation*', given at Munich University in 1927, in which all the various strands of his preoccupation, his reading of the past and his vision for the future, are united, not in any desire to establish a 'philosophy of art'—an intention which Hofmannsthal always disclaimed with firmness—but as an evocation of the 'healing function of language' in the social life of the nation.

The calamity of German politics (in contrast to France, a nation gathered around a firm intellectual centre of gravity) can, he suggests, be attributed to the fact that the German intellectual, above all the writer, must always seek, each on his own, in a thousand different ways, an escape out of seclusion and dissociation. How to overcome this sense of isolation and the hiatus which it has produced between the practical political life of the nation and its spiritual aspirations, that is the problem.

Hofmannsthal quotes Karl Vossler's words of 'the sociability of literature which closes the ring between poet and nation, writer and reader, speaker and listener' and pleads for a new relationship where the intellectual life is integrated into the social life of the community and where those who possess intellectual and moral authority do not stand aside from the pursuit of politics. *'Das Schrifttum als geistiger Raum der Nation'* was his final appeal for allegiance to a body politic, national and supra-national, resting not on power and force (whether the massive, static pressure of an existing order or the upheaval of violent revolution), not on ideology but on ideas, a living organism rooted in tradition, in a higher order, one which is above time and common to all its members, giving them a common language and knitting them together.

The attempt to represent on the stage these ultimate social questions, and to demonstrate the answer in dramatic action, made the tragedy *Der Turm* the centre and main preoccupation of Hofmannsthal's work in the closing years of his life.

IX

In *Jedermann* (1911) the devil is made to exclaim

> Die Welt ist dumm, gemein und schlecht,
> Und geht Gewalt allzeit vor Recht.

> The world is stupid, mean and bad,
> and right from power ever drubbing had.

Under the impression of the upheavals which shook Central Europe in the years immediately after the 1914-1918 war, as he witnessed the downfall of the established civil order and with it the progressive disintegration of the spiritual structure, Hofmannsthal, in *Das grosse Salzburger Welttheater* (1922), had undertaken once again to evoke and display, in the theatre, a larger view of the essence of humanity above the confusion of contemporary experience. In his final great tragedy, *Der Turm*, he returned, with ever greater anxiety and insight, to the search for a solution of the power struggle raging at all levels of the human community, a society rapidly losing its coherence, a common faith in common values. In fact, almost every scene of this historical play can be projected into political reality, and the picture of a world in which 'Power and Justice, the two mainstays of our social existence, are locked in gigantic battle' reveals a terrible and terrifying, sometimes even prophetic, likeness with our most recent past.

The exposition of the drama's plot, taken once more from Calderon, this time from his *La vida es sueño,* is simple enough. Its setting is a semi-historical, quint-essential Poland during the time of its deepest decline in the seventeenth century, and its central figure is Sigismund, the heir to the throne. A prophecy that the young prince will set his foot on his father's neck has led Basilius the King, in fear, to cast his son into a dreadful dungeon and to keep him there, like a wild beast, to rot behind ten-foot-thick walls.

In the appalling crime committed on the innocent child by his father's abuse of parental and regal authority, Hofmannsthal sees the curse of power destitute of moral strength and courage. Sigismund's cage is the thraldom of all those who labour and are heavy laden; the dungeon, *Der Turm,* thus represents in the poet's own words 'the hub of the world's injustice; here horrible injustice begets ceaselessly new monsters, as the carrion breeds flies'. All the major actors in the drama (a world exclusively of men) are tainted with this evil: Basilius the despotic King, full of suspicion and fear; Count Julian, the guardian of the tower, unable to resist the lure of power and ambition; the leaders of the revolutionary mob who have nothing to lose from turning 'everything upside down'; and 'the nameless ones who pray not and pay not' and follow only out of bewildered resentment, the very element which prevents the tortured kingdom from finding rest. All—with the exception perhaps of Oliver, the satanic corporal, for whom blind force and wanton lust hold their own satisfaction—all are able, at least for a moment, to see the good, but they can use it only as a tool, they have not the moral strength to hold it. Power is their corrupter, death and destruction their harvest.

Hofmannsthal's setting is terrifyingly concrete: a confused, brutalised, chaotic country utterly out of joint, recalling Central Europe after the scourge of the Thirty Years' War. This background of corruption, of riot and arson, of anarchy and murder, serves to throw into relief the noble character of the young prince Sigismund, the champion of pure love against power and violence, as well as the two other (minor) figures in *Der Turm* who are exponents of the author's positive ideas: the doctor and the servant Anton. Anton is a miniature sketch of the humble 'man of the people' with his unfailing simple sense

54

for the true and the spurious. Hofmannsthal obviously spent a great deal of affectionate care on him. The doctor too, although he plays no great part in the unfolding of the action, nevertheless holds an important place in the margin of the play.

It has been suggested that the character of the doctor might be looked upon as a marginal portrait of the poet who pictures himself, in the manner of the old masters, standing unobtrusively in a corner of his painting, not merely creator of the spectacle but participant also. The idea is a happy one: surrounded by conflict and chaos, Hofmannsthal saw in his work increasingly an execution of his mission as teacher and healer. Just as, in *Das kleine Welttheater,* the doctor watches over the madman and explains, out of deep, profoundly melancholy understanding of the tragedy of humanity, the immanence of evil in all being, so in *Der Turm* his office is that of the seer as much as of the healer. His knowledge is not mere science but wisdom: he does not presume to effect the cure: 'to liberate the restorative forces, that is our calling; the end is in higher hands'.

In this figure of the doctor Hofmannsthal proves once more that his analysis, however severe, is never pathological but therapeutic. 'To point out evil wherever we meet it, that is our charge', he says; by bringing it to light, he brings home the necessity of choice and responsibility. This is his diagnosis of Julian: 'You repudiate your heart. Heart and head must be one, yet you have consented in the satanic divorce'. Thus it is he who first brings out the full enormity of the crime which is being perpetrated against Sigismund: 'The spot where this life is torn from its roots will prove a whirling vortex which will drag us all to our doom', he exclaims, and in this way procures the first brief respite of freedom for the prisoner.

The young prince is brought back to the Court and there made aware of his true identity. The hope of breaking the vicious circle of injustice, fear and revenge, the sole prospect of peace based on a just order, now depends on his capacity to rise above his suffering and to overcome hatred and hardness of heart. In Calderon's play the prince, after his incarceration, is seen as man reverted to his natural savage state. The turning point comes only after he has learnt, back once more in his dungeon, that life is only dream. Thus the consciousness of the ephemeral, passing nature of this existence becomes the decisive spur to ethical action:

I desire not borrowed greatness
Nor imaginary glories.
Pomps fantastical, illusions
· · · · · ·
Cheats avail with me no longer,
Undeceived now I know surely
That our life is only a dream.

And again:

But well doing most imports me
Be it thus or thus: — if truth,
For truth's sake; if the other,
To win friends against the time
When this fleeting dream is over.

Hofmannsthal's problem, in writing *Der Turm,* was to find a solution as valid for his own time as that given by the great Catholic playwright of the Baroque for his in *La vida es sueño.* Sigismund, his sensitivity sharpened, his compassion widened as they only can be by infinite suffering, through self-conquest and self-perfection, has made himself a fit ruler; love renders him fit for power. The two scenes in which first the King, his father, and then Julian, his only friend, endeavour to tempt him are the culmination of Hofmannsthal's tragedy. Basilius offers him absolute power and urges him, as his first action, to put his mentor Julian to death as a dangerous conspirator; Sigismund throws away the sword and humiliates the King. More subtle is the temptation into which the prince is led by the cold calculating Julian: at the head of the revolt which Julian himself has fanned, Sigismund is to ride into the lawless land to out-power force with force. The suggestion may be regarded as politically expedient or even necessary, but once more, recognising that the very grounds on which Julian offers him kingship are deeply tainted, the young prince refuses to budge: 'I will have no hand in your machinations!'

It was at this stage that Hofmannsthal found himself face to face, once more, at the most crucial point, with his antithesis between Being and Becoming, between the will to act and the supreme solemnity of passive non-action. In publishing the first fragments of *Der Turm,* composed in the early years of the century, the poet spoke (in 1910) of the 'growing recognition, as I probed more deeply into my subject, of a central, almost insuperable difficulty, more of an intellectual-spiritual than of

an artistic-technical nature', which caused him to abandon the
work at this point, as he thought for good.

But the subject had taken too strong a hold of him. When
he took up *Der Turm* again in the years following the first
world war, he had gained new insight but not yet found the
answer which fully satisfied him. Are the force and example
of love and suffering alone strong enough to overcome evil and
restore order to the strife-torn realm? Or must the fight be
carried into the world? Between 1923 and 1927 the poet
produced two different, complete and apparently finished versions of his tragedy in which he proposed divergent, indeed in
some sense contrasting, solutions. In the first, when the people,
risen against oppression and arbitrary power, come to relieve
him from the dungeon and clamour for him to lead them to true
freedom, Sigismund goes out to fight. As commander of their
army, as 'the Poor Man's King before whom they carry the
sword and the scales', he suppresses lawlessness and strife
by force of arms because

Es ist noch die Zeit nicht, dass ihr mein sanftes Gesicht sehet.

The time is not yet to show my gentle face.

Although Sigismund does not survive his victory, the continuity
of his high conception of the dignity of power is assured by
the appearance on the stage, at the last moment, of the child-king
with his procession, symbol of the hopes of the rising generations,
a *deus ex coelo*.

Hofmannsthal was himself aware that this introduction of
the figure of the '*Kinderkönig*', which can only be taken
eschatologically as a divine promise of eventual conciliation,
was a foreign body which deprived his tragedy of its artistic
unity, 'at best a penultimate solution'. Thus, in the revised
version which appeared a few years later, these 'twelve legions
of angels' are dispensed with, and now the final words of the
dying Sigismund

Gebet Zeugnis, ich war da, wenngleich mich niemand gekannt hat.

Bear witness I was among you; even though none recognised me.

go out directly to the spectators themselves with the call:
'Go and be like him'. This attempt to give the audience a message
to carry into their own lives and to rouse them immediately to

a sense of their own responsibility, instead of directing them to higher forces at work outside this existence and to justice in another life, is far closer to Hofmannsthal's mature thought and to the constant endeavour of his work for the theatre than the conclusion of the earlier version.

But the revision went further still. No longer does Sigismund set out from his dungeon to pacify his country by force of arms. The representative of spiritual integrity and all the positive elements in man remains to the last unsullied by violence. The ultimate purpose of this Messianic figure now is not to bring peace to the world himself but to show the right way by which this peace can be found. It is not through action, but through the strength of his faith in man and his capacity to transmute suffering into creative energy, that the deadlock is broken. Sigismund's non-action is the great decisive action of his life. He seeks order, seeks to rally the forces of order against the onslaught of nihilism and chaos, yet he does not desire domination over others, but for each man dominion over himself.

Thus the image of the tower assumes yet another meaning, this time a positive one, as the tower of that spiritual strength which is in pure love, compassion and suffering. Sigismund says:

Ja, das bin ich, Herr und König auf immer in diesem festen Turm.

King and Master I shall be for ever in this strong Tower.

And this is how one of the peasants addresses him:

> Du hast uns gezeigt: Gewalt, unwiderstehliche, und
> über der Gewalt ein Höheres, davon wir den Namen nicht
> wissen und so bist du unser Herr geworden, der eine, der
> einzige, ein Heiligtum, unzugänglich.

> You have shown us something higher that is above power,
> something we cannot name, and so you have become our
> master, the one and only, sacred to us and unreachable.

When the prince exclaims, just before he is treacherously killed,

> Ich bin allein und sehne mich verbunden zu sein

> I am alone and long to be united

he is looking forward, we know, to the only union which now remains—that with God.

In the very year which saw the first publication of the completed tragedy, there were also published in the German orbit both Kafka's *Der Prozess* and Hitler's *Mein Kampf*—the one the most relentless parable of the working of irrational fear and anonymous power, the other a call for its most ruthless exploitation. This juxtaposition accentuates the significance and the urgency of Hofmannsthal's struggle in *Der Turm* to counter and overcome the imminence of chaos by setting against it his awareness of a higher, timeless moral order. It is a long road which leads from the aloofness of the precocious young 'aesthete' Loris to this almost desperate attempt of the later Hofmannsthal to come to grips directly with the paramount problems of his time. This is how he responded with his whole personality to the changes of the period through which he lived. His determination to break the circle of isolation and loneliness which had surrounded his adolescence, admirable decision of the will which helped him to close the arid cleavage between imagination and life, had opened the way to an even richer unfolding of his art, and gave it that wider authority which is only now making itself felt.

'I am perhaps an all-too-social person—I take seriously the living-together of human beings', Hofmannsthal wrote late in life to his friend Carl Burckhardt. 'Taking it seriously' meant to him more than the duty not to stand aside from the problems of his time; it was an obligation, increasingly compelling, to take part, in his own sphere and within his limits, in shaping it. 'The "I" is inextricably mixed up in the affairs of the world —that is its curse but also its unique God-given chance of exaltation and fulfilment'. Hofmannsthal knew that he could never become a 'popular' writer; his link with the 'popular' even in the sense in which he used the term was in fact far more tenuous than he was willing to admit to himself. He realised that his was a voice crying in the wilderness, yet he never raised it in anger or in lament, and there is no trace of cynicism in his utterances.

His answer was to be of this world *and* of that other greater order of which it is but a part. Thus he faced the living issues raised in Europe by the outcome of the first world war and the wider implications of the eternal struggle for power in the social and international sphere with its recurrent destructive effects. Petrified and fascinated at the same time by the terrible task of

59

representing in *Der Turm* 'the irruption of the forces of chaos into an order no longer upheld and supported by the power of the spirit', Hofmannsthal allowed this tragedy (on which he was at work, at intervals, for almost a quarter-century) to become the dominating and often torturing preoccupation of his closing years.

What was at stake here for him was, as Carl Burckhardt has pointed out, far more than the success or failure of a work of art; it was an attempt not to escape from reality, however brutal it may be, but, on the contrary, intellectually and spiritually to master the intolerable and apparently inexorable unfolding of events. Once he had set out on this task, Hofmannsthal, being the man he was, had to go all the way. It is not only the testimony of his friends that bears witness to the poet's heroic struggle with his subject; the tragedy itself is proof enough: the sentences of immense weight, desperately, often labouriously wrought; the heavy atmosphere of corroding evil which pervades the work, the ambivalence of the two alternative closing acts with their contrasting solutions. 'The walls are shaken in their foundations and our way is lost in impassable terrain', says one of the characters in *Der Turm*. Hofmannsthal had long ago learnt that in order to understand the calamity and the suffering of the world in which he lived he had to be fully involved in it, but he also knew that in order to give it shape and form he would have to lift himself out of this involvement and to rise above it. 'Lost in impassable terrain' —it meant also the recognition that he had tried to put into a stage play more than it could be expected to hold. 'The final act', he wrote, 'has something of a castle built over an abyss. One cannot, after all, give more than in one lies.'

It would have been a good last word. 'The end is in higher hands', says the doctor in *Der Turm*. Hofmannsthal was willing to carry the search for the healing forces, which alone can reconcile us to the tragic aspect of the human condition, to another level, into a world beyond, to a Divine Saviour, to a God of Love. His work after the first world war shows a gradual steady assimilation of ideals and conceptions of the Christian religion, indeed of the Christian Church. To that end his work converged; from the immanent mystical experience of his pagan adolescence he arrived, in ripe manhood, at a conscious re-conquest of comparable assurance through an active faith. It is reported by those who were close to Hofmannsthal in the last years of his life that he confessed that he was, on occasion, experiencing moments of 'total apprehension of God'. With this knowledge of the immanent presence of the divine he represented in his final great work that which, in the last resort, can never be understood except in the certainty of visionary knowledge. Even to the poet himself this was only granted at rare moments of elevation. At other times Hofmannsthal was alternately tortured and spurred on by the intellectual inadequacy (for so they must seem) of the solutions he had found to the questions raised in his tragedy. With the figure of Sigismund, which he recast again and again, he struggled longer and more painfully than with any other of his creations; in him he had intended to embody, to make visible and to communicate his faith in the unconquerable spirit of man, and to recall, in defiance of the double threat of nihilism and materialism, the road to that freedom which is within ourselves.

His aim had been to show Sigismund's bloodless triumph over force, but his heart misgave him: the young prince, unsullied, is struck down by the evil which, to all appearance, he had conquered for ever. That is the fable of the play. Can the good, the pure, the true prevail only in the life of the mind and must they inevitably fail in contact with the dark forces of this world? Must action necessarily lead to this, even if it is the fruit of so long and so painful a process of conscious 'becoming', of so much heart-searching, suffering, and pure striving?

These difficulties, these doubts which are ours, Hofmannsthal must have carried with him for years, and we can but marvel how he found the strength to live so long with—indeed within— a subject so grave, so nightmarish, always battling for a solution. It has in fact been suggested that it was this burden, and the constant, unrelenting sense of personal responsibility, which eventually killed him. And so, when at the age of 55 he suddenly and quite unexpectedly died in the midst of his struggle to secure in this world a habitation for the spirit, it was found that he had expressed the wish to be buried in the cassock of a Franciscan friar.

FINAILHOF
MADONA DI SENALES

July—September 1954

BIOGRAPHICAL AND
BIBLIOGRAPHICAL NOTES

Hugo von Hofmannsthal was born in Vienna on February 1st, 1874, the son of a Viennese banker. While still at school he attracted attention and admiration with poems and occasional essays which he published under the pseudonym 'Loris'. He studied first law, then Romance philology at Vienna University and submitted there, in 1901, a habilitation thesis, a study of the development of Victor Hugo, with the intention of adopting an academic career. The application was eventually withdrawn.

Hofmannsthal lived all his life in or near Vienna, after his marriage (in 1902) at Rodaun, a few miles from the city, where he was often visited by his close friends, among them E. v. Bodenhausen, Rudolf Alexander Schroeder and, in later years, Carl J. Burckhardt. The letters which he exchanged with these friends, with Stefan George, with Richard Strauss and others, are of considerable interest and literary importance. Apart from occasional travels in Western Europe (twice for a short stay in England), Italy and Greece, his life was outwardly uneventful. After the first world war, Hofmannsthal was instrumental, with Max Reinhardt and others, in founding the Salzburg Festival. Occasionally, but not often, he appeared as speaker on public occasions.

In July 1929, at the age of fifty-five, Hofmannsthal suddenly died at Rodaun of a cerebral stroke following upon the suicide of one of his sons. A considerable amount of his work, including his only novel, the fragment *Andreas,* was posthumously published, and the publication of his literary remains is not yet completed. Hofmannsthal's statue at Salzburg was demolished by the Nazis in 1938; his books were boycotted.

A very large number of essays and studies of individual aspects of his work have been published in recent years, but there is not yet a major comprehensive critical study. Of the personal recollections the most perceptive and sympathetic are those of Jacob Wassermann, *Hofmannsthal der Freund* (1929), and of Carl J. Burckhardt, *Erinnerungen an Hofmannsthal* (1943). On the occasion of the 25th anniversary of Hofmannsthal's death, the President of the West German Federal Republic, Professor Theodor Heuss, gave a memorial address at Bad Hersfeld, paying profound tribute to Hofmannsthal's work, which is now more widely read in German-speaking countries than ever before.

BRIEF LIST OF HOFMANNSTHAL'S PUBLISHED WORKS

A complete edition of Hofmannsthal's Works in fifteen volumes, edited by Herbert Steiner, is now in course of publication by the S. Fischer Verlag, Frankfurt am Main. Twelve volumes have so far appeared.

ENGLISH TRANSLATIONS:

Electra, translation by Alfred Kalisch, 1908.
The Rose-Bearer, translated by the same, 1912.
Ariadne, translated by the same, 1912.
 (These three translations are very poor and convey no impression of the original.)
Hofmannsthal's *Everyman* exists in two English versions, the first by George Sterling, published in 1917, another published 1933.
The Fool and Death, a metrical translation by H. E. Mierow, 1930.
Andreas, translated by Mary Hottinger, 1936.
Selected Prose of Hugo von Hofmannsthal, translated by Mary Hottinger and Tania and James Stern, 1952.